Chester County
Cookery

Chester County
Cookery

Compiled and edited by Virginia Penrose

ILLUSTRATED BY CÉCILE NEWBOLD BARNETT

COPYRIGHT 1950, BY ST. PAUL'S CHURCH
WEST WHITELAND, CHESTER COUNTY
PENNSYLVANIA, U.S.A.

ALL PROCEEDS FROM THE SALE OF THIS BOOK
ARE FOR THE BENEFIT
OF THIS EPISCOPAL CHURCH, FOUNDED IN 1828,
IN THE HISTORIC CHESTER VALLEY

SET UP AND PRINTED IN THE UNITED STATES OF AMERICA
BY PRINCETON UNIVERSITY PRESS, PRINCETON, N.J., U.S.A.

CONTENTS

Appetizers	15
Soups	21
Fish	33
Entrees and Meat	43
Sauces	69
Game and Fowl	79
Eggs and Cheese	89
Vegetables	99
Salads	115
Breads	127
Cakes	139
Desserts	165
Beverages	191
Preserves	201
Miscellaneous	221
Contributors	251
Index	253

BY WAY OF INTRODUCTION

CHESTER COUNTY—that glorious rolling countryside in Eastern Pennsylvania whose hills and valleys, woodlands and streams and quiet ponds, whose clover meadows and tilled fields and green pastures with nearby red barns and silos and herds, and whose stone farmhouses and spotless dairy buildings all show what *the best traditions of farming and husbandry* can mean—it is *in Chester County*, fox hunting country of the East, that *Cooking and Cookery* come into their own!

This truly is an historic land—where Washington wintered at Valley Forge, where he fought along banks of the placid Brandywine. It is a countryside famed for hospitality of its bounteous table. William Penn made such pleasant discovery, in the early 1700's.

This book, now happily your personal property, seeks to record for you and for posterity some of the finest of Chester County's Cookery!

To bring you closer to that rich farming area, you will find illustrations herein of some of the places and things that are *symbols* of the wholesome, outdoor life by which Chester County is blessed.

Come to Chester County yourself and let us show you our treasures—including Cookery!

APPETIZERS

Red Caviar

To one jar of red caviar, add the oil from a small can of anchovies. Mix well and chill. Serve cold on small rounds of thin toast.

Use the anchovies for butter spread or mix with scrambled eggs. VP

Herb Butter

Cream one-fourth pound butter. Add a teaspoon each, finely chopped basil, chives, parsley, marjoram, thyme. Mix well. Allow to age for a couple of hours. Use on fresh crackers or toast fingers.

Snappy Cheese Biscuit

Same amount of butter as cheese. Enough flour to hold—as little as possible. Dash of paprika. Roll like pie crust and cut in small discs (size of quarter) and bake 8 or 10 minutes. Serve with cocktails.

Cherry Codfish Balls

1 cup codfish
2 cups potatoes
1 egg
¼ cup cream

Put codfish in cold water and bring to boil, drain and cover with cold water again and simmer until tender. Strain and put through food chopper. Boil potatoes and put through ricer and mix with codfish. Add beaten egg and cream. Drop by spoonfuls into very hot fat for one minute. These balls should be about the size of a cherry and should be served on toothpicks.
VP

Foie Gras Maison Potter

Prepare a whole goose liver, by taking out the nerves, etc., season with salt and pepper. Put in a frying pan, saute in butter. Then place in a pottery casserole that has been well warmed. Save the gravy in which the liver has been cooked and add one glass of good sauterne, add some veal stock, mix, then pour over the liver, in the casserole. Put the lid on and cook for about an hour, at a low temperature.
CPR—Karlsbad, Dec. 9, 1932

MEMORANDA

MEMORANDA

SOUPS

Onion Soup

2 large onions or 4 small ones. Slice them and fry in ¼ pound butter until very brown. Pour over 1 quart stock—one cup of toasted bread scraps. 2 tablespoons of grated cheese. Put in oven until bread scraps rise to surface and dry out.

STOCK

- 1 pound lean meat
- 1 pig or calf's foot
- 2 carrots
- 1 onion
- 2 leeks
- 1 turnip
- 3 quarts cold water

Cut up vegetables—let simmer slowly for 3 hours. Strain and put on ice. Add salt when finished. CPR

Onion Soup

4 large mild onions (some say ½ pound per person) sliced thinly; 4 tablespoons butter or chicken fat or both. Fry out onions until slightly brown. Add 1 quart chicken broth and 1 teaspoon Worcestershire sauce. Salt and pepper. Simmer for 40 minutes. Toast thick slices of bread (without crust) and serve with lots of Parmesan cheese. VP

Philadelphia Pepper Pot

    1 knuckle of veal
    1 pound of plain tripe
    1 pound of honey-comb tripe
  bunch of pot herbs
    1 onion—chopped
    ¼ pound suet
    2 med-sized potatoes
    1 bay leaf
    3 quarts of cold water
    2 tablespoons of butter
    2 tablespoons of flour
  salt and cayenne to taste

Wash the tripe well in cold water. Put in a kettle, cover with cold water and boil 8 hours. This should be cooked the day before you want the soup. Wipe the knuckle with a damp towel, put it in a soup kettle, cover with the water, place on the fire and bring slowly to a SIMMER carefully skimming off the scum. Simmer gently for three hours, then strain and return soup to kettle. Wash the pot herbs, chop the parsley, rub off the thyme leaves, and cut only half the red pepper (they would put a whole one in each bunch). Cut the tripe into pieces one inch square. Cut the meat from the knuckle into small pieces; add these also to the soup; place it on the fire and when at the boiling point, season with salt and cayenne. Rub the butter and flour together and stir into the boiling soup, and then fifty small dumplings made as follows: Chop the suet fine, measure it, and take double the quantity of flour, one-quarter of teaspoon of salt, mix well together, moisten with ice water (about a quarter of a cup). Form into tiny dumplings about the size of a marble, throw into the soup. Simmer for 15 minutes and serve.   VP

Mulligatawny Soup

    1 large onion
    1 tablespoon Curry powder
    2 tablespoons flour
    1 carrot
    2 apples
    2 quarts good stock
    1 gill milk
    1 gill cream

Fry onion till brown, add curry and cook slowly for ten minutes, add flour and vegetables with stock and milk. Cook for one hour and pass through hair sieve. Add cream at the last. Serve with sippets or boiled rice.   CPR

Bouquet Garni

1 tablespoon each thyme, marjoram, dried parsley, sage, grated dried lemon rind, celery seed, and 6 bay leaves. Place in cheesecloth bag and remove when desired flavor is achieved.

Cream of Mushroom Soup

One veal shin bone, cracked, and boiled in two quarts water for 8 hours. 1 pound mushrooms, chopped very fine and boiled in double boiler with enough water to cover for 8 hours.

Just before serving combine ingredients in the proportion of one cup stock, one cup mushrooms and one cup cream. Salt and pepper and large lump of butter. Thicken slightly if desired.   **VP**

Vichysoisse

    4 large potatoes halved
    3 sliced leeks—use only white
    1 clove garlic

Boil in water to cover gently. When potatoes are tender put all through ricer. Add 2 tablespoons butter, ½ teaspoon salt, a litle pepper, 2 cups coffee cream (light).

Mix thoroughly and chill for several hours.

Serve with chopped chives.

If too thick, thin with milk.   **VP**

Emergency Soups

    1 can Campbell's green turtle soup
    1 can Campbell's pea soup
    Sherry

    1 can Campbell's tomato soup
    1 can Campbell's pea soup
    Sherry

Okra Soup

    1 can okra—slice and add to
    1 can Campbell's consomme
    Sherry
    Small amount of Vigor or Bovril   CPR

Barley Soup

Take cup barley, wash it. Cover with lukewarm water (1 quart) and let simmer for three hours. Strain with potato masher, pour back and strain again. Season with salt and pepper and ½ tablespoon butter. Let simmer until ready. Warm milk separately and add at the last moment.

Peanut Butter Soup

1 tablespoonful smooth peanut butter to each cup of milk used. Dissolve peanut butter in small quantity of warm milk before adding it to boiling milk. Boil till consistency of thick cream. Season to taste.   MC

Fish Chowder

Take a 7 or 8 pound haddock and have the market remove skin, bones and head and wrap separately from the filets. Cover the bones with about 2 quarts of water and cook slowly all night on a coal range or about 6 or 8 hours. Mince half pound salt pork and fry till delicately brown and remove from pot. A big iron pot is best for chowder. Cut fine 4 or 6 onions and sauté in fat until soft. Pour off excess fat. Strain liquor from bones into pot. Add 4 or 6 potatoes diced small. Cut filet of fish into half-inch pieces and add to pot. Add water to make about two or three quarts of soup. Add the salt pork. Let simmer for 40 minutes, add the salt and pepper to taste, a lump of butter and just before serving 1 cup of thin cream. Serve with common crackers.

This chowder is a meal and is usually accompanied by slaw and pie.   VP

Clam Chowder

    1 quart medium sized clams
    ¼ pound salt pork
    4 medium sized onions
    4 small potatoes
    2 slim carrots, diced
    3 good sized tomatoes
    1 stalk of celery, diced
    1 quart of water
    ½ Bay leaf
    ¼ teaspoon thyme
    Parsley, salt and pepper

Chop the onions fine, combine with diced salt pork and cook over low fire until onions are tender. Add peeled and chopped tomatoes, carrots, celery, a minced sprig of parsley, the bay leaf, thyme, water, and pepper as liked. Cover and simmer an hour and three quarters. After it has simmered an hour add the potatoes, diced. Strain the juice from the clams through cheesecloth. Chop clams and mix with the strained juice. Add to the chowder and cook 15 minutes more. Remove the bay leaf and parsley. Add salt if required. Serve piping hot with oyster crackers.   EG

Clam Chowder

    1 pt. clams
    3 potatoes
    3 onions

⅛ lb. salt pork—try out and remove—fry onions in fat—cut potatoes and flour well, add water to cover potatoes, boil 5 minutes, add clams and boil 3 minutes—add top of bottle of milk and heat.   VP

Steam 1 dozen medium size clams until shells open
Strain liquid to use in making chowder
Fry 2 slices salt pork and one slice onion until brown (all minced)
Add 2 cups sliced potatoes
Clams cut into small pieces
Boil until potatoes are tender
2 cups milk, heat but do not boil
Butter and seasonings before serving   ENT

Tomato-Crab Soup

    2 cans tomato soup   1 large can crab meat
    2 cans milk

Combine ingredients and heat well. Place tablespoon whipped cream on top—sprinkle with paprika.

Cream Mushroom Soup

    1 can cream of mushroom soup
    1 can cream of spinach soup
    2 cans beef bouillon or 3 cubes dissolved in three cups water

Mix well, add a bouquet of fresh rosemary, sage to this soup and simmer one hour. Remove herbs, add salt and pepper and a lump of butter.   CPR

Dumplings for Soup

Grate good sized cold cooked potato (warm mashed ones will do)
    1 egg
    Add shortening from top of soup while boiling
    1 teaspoon salt   2 cups sifted flour

Stir together with milk to make thick.
Drop by small spoonfuls to boiling soup—do not cover while cooking.
Done when they rise to top of soup.

Try these once and you will never want any other.

Sorrel Soup

Cut up sorrel. Melt butter and add sorrel. Let it get soft but not brown. Add chicken stock at the last moment. Add an egg yolk and a little cream if desired.

SORREL FOR SOUP—pick early in Autumn and dry in dehydrator.   CPR

Potage Germiny

Cook with butter, covered, until soft, ½ pound of leaves of sorrel shredded. Pass through a fine sieve and add 1½ quarts of white stock (chicken or veal). This is the base.

Just before serving add a liaison of yolks of 10 eggs diluted with ½ pint of cream.

Prepare this by adding a little cream, cold, to the eggs, and then a little of the other cream heated to boiling point, and then the remainder gradually. When completed bring to the boiling point, then strain and just before serving add to the stock, bring to boiling point and then complete the soup off the fire by adding 5 oz. of butter and shredded chervil or sorrel cooked in butter for five minutes. Then serve. CPR

MEMORANDA

MEMORANDA

MEMORANDA

FISH

Oysters Supreme

    3 dozen large oysters
    ¾ cup cream
    1 tablespoon flour
    1 tablespoon olive oil
    1 onion minced
    1 tablespoon butter
    1 clove garlic
    parsley, chives and a dash of mace

Cook oysters slightly and cut, *not* mince
Combine in long flat pyrex dish—bake in hot oven 25 minutes
CPR

Sole

Take thin slices of filet of sole. Wash and fry slices of filet in iron pan. Squeeze lemon over each slice. Put big lump of butter on each slice. Season with salt and pepper. To every pound of filet pour ½ pint of heavy whipped cream. Put in oven for about 20 minutes.
CPR

Haddock

Take filets of haddock—roll in flour then in butter. Add seasoning to flour and a little cream—add a cupful of butter.
CPR

Lobster a la Newburg

    5 pounds cooked lobster
    3 dozen yolks hard boiled eggs
    1 pound butter
    ½ pound flour
    2 quarts cream
    1 bottle sherry or madeira wine
    1 teaspoon grated nutmeg
salt and pepper to taste

Sprinkle wine over lobster meat—let stand 2 hours
Make sauce with butter, flour and cream
Press yolks to paste, add slowly to sauce, strain over lobster
Serve steaming hot

Newburg Sauce

    1 cup heavy cream
    1 tablespoon butter
    2 tablespoons flour
  yolks of 3 hard cooked eggs
    ½ cup sherry
  cayenne pepper and salt to taste

Heat cream very hot—add the flour and butter creamed together and the hard cooked egg yolks mashed fine. Cook together until thick then add the sherry and seasoning.   CPR

Sole Marguery

Smear deep pan with butter, salt and pepper. Put in fish, mushrooms and shrimps. Add one wine glass of white wine, lemon and a dash of water. Cook 10 minutes covered. Use about 6 small mushrooms sliced, 4 shrimps that have been boiled. Drain fish and put in dish. Pour over sauce Margueray. Reduce fish juice to about 2 tablespoons. Add 3 tablespoons Hollandaise, 3 tablespoons cream sauce (very thick), one tablespoon of fresh cream. More salt and pepper and lemon if necessary. Heat.   CPR

Salmon Puffles

- 1 cup medium white sauce
- 1 tablespoon scraped onion
- 1 tablespoon chopped parsley
- 2 chopped hard cooked eggs
- ½ teaspoon salt
- dash paprika
- 1 can salmon flaked (reserve ½ cup)

Make pie pastry and roll thin, cut into 6 five-inch squares. Place large spoonful mixture on each. Fold over, seal edges with fork. Make three slits on top of each—insert flake in each (from reserve), glaze top—bake in hot oven. Serve with apple rings.

APPLE RINGS

3 large cored apples cut in thirds. Place in baking pan, cover each with 2 tablespoons brown sugar, 1 tablespoon tomato catsup. Bake in moderate oven, turning often. EH

Boiled Salt Cod the Italian Way

Chuse a fine piece, and lay it to soak in a great deal of Water; when it is soaked, clean it thoroughly, and set it on in a large stewpan, with a great deal of very clean water; let it boil up once or twice, then set it off. Set on another stewpan with a good piece of butter, put to this a handful of parsley cut small, two cloves of garlick shred, and some thyme and sweet margoram leaves picked clean from the stalks; when these are warm together, take out the cod from the water in the other stewpan and lay it into this upon these ingredients; squeeze a large Seville orange over it, dust on a little pepper, and pour in half a gill of sweet and fine oil; set all over the fire, stir it frequently about, turn it two or three times, and taste it to find whether it be well relished, if not, add more pepper or more orange juice; then dish it up hot, and serve with it gravy, with essence of jam for those who chuse it. ATH

Shad Roe

MAIN LUNCHEON COURSE OR FIRST COURSE FOR DINNER—8 SERVINGS

    1½ Shad Roe—parboil and put through ricer
    6   eggs—well beaten
    1½ pints cream

Mix thoroughly and put in ring mold—in pan of hot water in moderate oven for about 30 minutes.

Serve with tomato sauce or the following, which is preferable:

    4 hard boiled eggs—chopped
    ¼ lb. butter
    1 stalk celery
    bunch parsley
    mustard chow chow, little more than pint
    sugar and seasonings to taste   CPR

Cod Sounds

Lay the cod sounds, which are taken from the inside of the fish, near the backbone, in a clean earthen dish, pour on them two quarts of scalding hot water, not boiling; when they have lain a few minutes, take them out, rub them well with salt, throw them into the hot water again, and after they have lain three or four minutes more, take off the blackish skin, and all that looks disagreeable about them; this is called blanching the sounds.

Throw them into a saucepan of cold water, and let them simmer till they are tender. Take them out of the saucepan, dry them in a cloth, flour them well, and broil them. While they are broiling make the following sauce: Set on a quarter of a pint of gravy in a small saucepan, stir in two teaspoonfuls of mustard, and sprinkle in a little pepper and salt; this is to be set over the fire till hot, and then put in a piece of butter rolled in flour, and boil all up together that it may be well mixed; lay the sounds in a dish and pour this sauce over them.   ATH

Shrimp Creole

Chop one pepper and several onions and fry in small amount of bacon fat. Add one large can tomatoes and cook slowly for an hour. Add one pound peeled shrimps and cook ½ hour. Serve with rice. VP

Crab Meat

Ring mold filled with tomato jelly with crab meat in center—mayonnaise dressing. CPR

To Fry Smelts

Put into a deep soup dish a quart of vinegar, break in four bay leaves, put in a nutmeg shaved, not grated, four bruised cloves, some pepper and salt, and a few chives chopped, not very small. This is a marinade for the smelts and vastly improves their flavor. Lay the smelts, cleaned, in this liquor, and turn them once in a quarter of an hour; let them lie in it an hour and a half, and then take them out; wipe them very dry with a napkin, dredge them well with flour and fry them. They will thus be of a fine brown, very delicate and will have all their own rich and elegant flavor vastly improved by the marinade. Some serve with a gravy sauce for them, and others a shrimp sauce, but this is all wrong; if it be any one's particular fancy to have such a sauce, let it be served separate in a sauce boat, not in the dish with the smelts. This dish should be garnished with crisp parsley, and nothing should be eat with the smelts but salt. ATH

MEMORANDA

MEMORANDA.

MEMORANDA

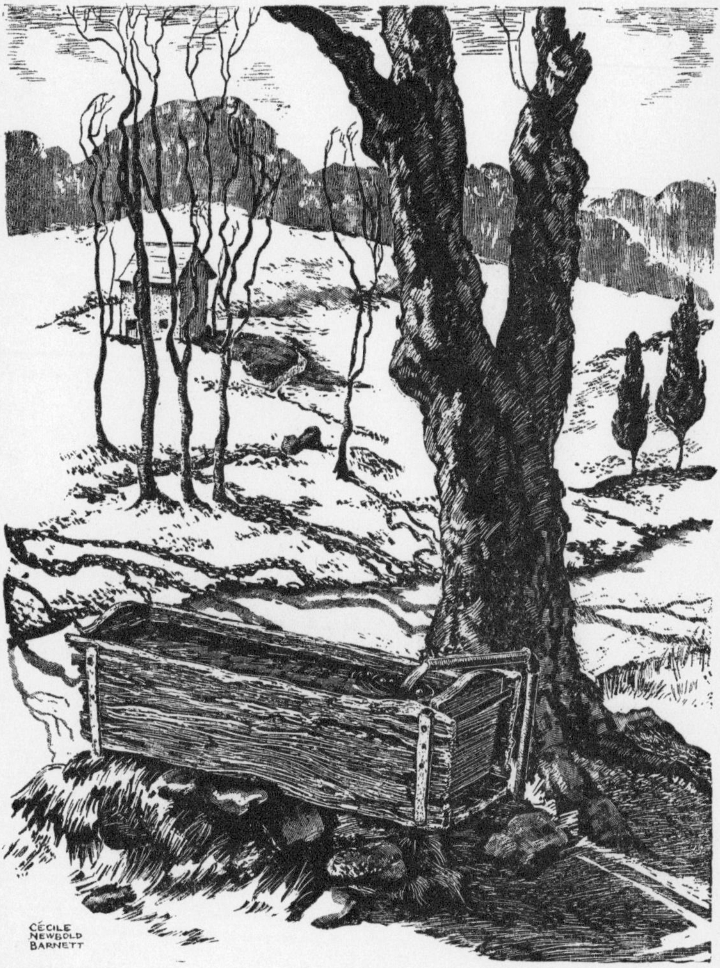
CÉCILE
NEWBOLD
BARNETT

ENTREES & MEAT

Reading Noodles
2 eggs
3 cups flour

Made into a dough with a mixture of one-half milk and one-half water. The dough a little heavier than that for pancakes. Use no salt.

When the dough is ready slice it with a knife from a paddle into boiling water which is pretty salty, boil for a few moments only and then drain.

Meanwhile have prepared the following. Fry a cut onion in some lard until brown, drain off the lard and throw away the onion, to the lard add an equal quantity of butter and melt the whole, pouring the hot sauce over the Reading noodles.

These noodles are also excellent if fried like potatoes.

The water in which the noodles have been boiled makes an excellent soup if a few noodles are left in it, about half the water thrown away, and made up with milk to suit the taste.

These noodles are also good when boiled in chicken broth.

CPR

An Onion Pie

This, though we commonly call it an onion pie, is made of a mixture of potatoes, onions, and apples, and they ought to be in equal quantities to give it a good taste. Boil about a pound and half of potatoes, and when they are pretty well done, peel them and cut them into slices, peel the same quantity of onions, and cut them also into slices, and pare some apples, cut them in the same manner into slices, taking out the cores. When the ingredients are thus ready make a good crust, and cover a dish with it; break a quarter of pound of butter into small pieces, and distribute this over the crust; and then make the following seasoning: grate down a whole nutmeg, bruise a quarter of an ounce of mace, mix these together, and add a teaspoonful of pepper and three teaspoonfuls of salt; mix all these together, and strew some of it over the bottom. Then lay in a covering of the potatoes, onions, and apples interchangeably, a slice of one and a slice of another. Then lay in the yolks of four eggs boiled hard. Upon these lay in some potatoes by themselves, then some onions, and at top some apples. Dust in some of the seasoning as every parcel is put in. Mix half a dozen more hard yolks of eggs in different parts of the pie, and also half a pound of butter broken into scraps. When all is thus in, spread over the upper layer some butter, and scatter on the remainder of the spices. Cover up the pie, and send it to the oven, first pouring in a quarter of a pint of water. As the potatoes are boiled before they are put in, half an hour in moderately hot oven will do the pie. It is to be served hot. ATH

Pork Cake

Put 1 pound fat pork through grinder. Pour over it ½ pint boiling water. Add 1 pound chopped seeded raisins, 2 cups sugar, 2 teaspoons soda stirred into 1 cup molasses, 1 egg, ½ nutmeg grated, teaspoon each cinnamon, cloves and salt. Flour to make very stiff batter. Moderate oven. Decorate with citron if you wish.

Gnocchi Parisien

    1 cup boiling water
    ¼ pound butter
    salt and cayenne pepper
    ½ cup bread flour (scant)
    2 cups grated Parmesan cheese (1 for sauce—1 for paste)
    3 eggs

Melt the butter in the cup of boiling water. Add to this salt and pepper. When butter is melted take saucepan off fire and while still very hot, throw in flour all at once, stirring hard. When paste is perfectly smooth put back on low heat and stir until it dries a bit. Take off fire and cool. It does not need to be actually cold. Then stir in cheese and the unbeaten whole eggs one at a time (at this point taste mixture to see if it has enough seasoning and cheese). When mixture is cold put into a paste bag with an opening in the end of about the size of a ten cent piece. Have a large saucepan ready with boiling water salted. Hold the paste bag over the boiling water and squeeze out the mixture, cutting it off close to the end with a sharp knife in pieces of about an inch long. Let the pieces drop into the boiling water. They go to the bottom at first, then they swell and rise to the surface. Leave them in the boiling water for a moment after they float up, then take them out with a skimmer and drain. Put the gnocchi into a buttered baking dish, cover with white sauce of about the consistency of medium cream into which some cheese has been dissolved and put into the oven. Allow it to boil long enough to thicken cream sauce, then cover with buttered bread crumbs and brown under the broiler.　　　　　　　　　　　　　　　　CPR

Liver Loaf

    1 pound liver　　　　　　　add 1 egg
    1 pound salt pork　　　　　　½ cup thin cream
    1 onion　　　　　　　　　　salt and pepper
    4 soda crackers—ground　　Bake 1½ hours, slow oven
       four times　　　　　　　　　　　　　　　　EAC

Souffle a la Refrigerator

2 cups ham ground fine—no fat
  (use pickings from baked ham bone, roast beef or lamb or fish)
1 onion ground with meat
1 tablespoon prepared mustard (omit with fish and use lemon juice)
1 cup cooked rice, noodles, macaroni or bread crumbs
Dash of Worcestershire Sauce or wine
2 cups cream sauce
  (use chicken fat, oil or butter and cream, a little celery salt—3 tablespoons flour)

Combine ingredients, add yolks 4 eggs beaten and fold in whites of eggs beaten stiff. Put in greased ring mold and poach 45 to 60 minutes. Turn out on large platter and fill hollow with cooked peas, carrots, spinach or other vegetable.

Or add a little gelatin and put in loaf pan and slice when cold and serve with salad. For variety add grated cheese, or sautéed mushrooms or pimentos or chopped hard boiled eggs.

This preparation may be used for stuffing peppers which have been cleaned and let stand in hot salt water for 15 minutes. Bake 40 minutes. Serve with tomato sauce. VP

Pigs in Blankets

2½ pounds round steak, sliced thin
1 large onion
3 or 4 slices bacon
salt and pepper

Cut round steak into pieces about 3 inches square. On each place a little diced onion, bacon cut in small pieces, salt and pepper. Roll up and skewer with toothpicks. Brown in suet or bacon fat on all sides, then add a half cup of water, cover and simmer slowly for about 1 hour till tender. Thicken gravy and serve with the meat. JR

Ham Loaf

Grind 1½ cups of ham using both fat and lean. Mix with 1½ cups of cold cooked rice, 1 cup of grated soft bread crumbs, 1½ cups of cream sauce, 1 stalk of celery chopped fine, 1 large onion minced or ground, 2 chopped pimentos, 1 teaspoon minced parsley and seasonings to taste.

When they are well mixed, pack the mixture firmly in a buttered loaf bread pan. Set the pan in another pan with about one inch of warm water in the bottom. Bake one hour in a moderate (350°) oven.
EG,

Spaghetti SS "France" 1930

¾ pound spaghetti—cooked 12 minutes in boiling salted water. Drain and put half in hot dish—add large lump of butter, some Parmesan cheese grated and sauce. Alternate. Mix and add cheese on top. Serve with cheese and sauce.

SAUCE

    1 can concentrated tomato paste
    1 pound Parmesan cheese (keep in damp cloth, grate as needed)

To 1 can tomato paste, measure 3 cans cold water—put in double boiler—add 3 tablespoons olive oil, cayenne pepper, salt to taste. Bring to boil. Simmer for ¾ hour.
CPR

Spaghetti Sauce (Mexico City)

    1 can tomato sauce
    1 can tomato paste
    1 clove garlic

Put 4 tablespoons olive oil in pan, sizzle 1 clove garlic cut in small pieces until brown and remove. Add 1 pound ground beef and stir slightly. Add salt, pepper, a little chili powder, the tomato sauce and tomato paste. Cook gently for 20 minutes. Serve with plenty of grated cheese.
VP

Italian Spaghetti

1 package thin spaghetti cooked in salted boiling water until tender. Drain and place in greased baking dish.

SAUCE

    4 slices bacon—cut fine and browned slowly.
    1 large can tomatoes
    1 onion, cut fine
    1 clove garlic
    1 teaspoon dry mustard
    1 can chopped mushrooms
    salt and pepper
    1 green pepper chopped fine

Let come to boil. Pour over spaghetti and stir in ½ pound sharp cheese cut in small pieces. Bake in moderate oven 350° for thirty minutes.   EBT

Lamb Stew

Cut a shoulder of lamb in two-inch squares and remove all fat. Put in stew pot and add not over two cups of water, 2 bits of bay leaf, 4 whole cloves, ½ teaspoon whole pepper and simmer two hours. One hour before serving add salt and all or any of the following vegetables: one potato per person, 2 carrots, 1 onion; a bunch of celery cut in two-inch lengths; ½ pound of green beans left whole, 1 cup peas, lima beans, cucumber or eggplant cut in cubes. The liquor should be enough for gravy but not all watery. Serve with horse radish or relish.   VP

Force Meat

1 pound of lean veal—cut the sinews out and chop it fine
1 pound of beef suet—shred fine
An onion—chopped
Season with pepper, salt, mace, cloves, sweet herbs and parsley. The yolks of 2 eggs

[48]

Stuffed Cabbage

Remove the dead outside leaves of a large cabbage. Cut off a lid at the stalk end and hollow the cabbage. Do this with a sharp knife, but see to it that a sufficient number of leaves are left. Fill hollow with forcemeat. Replace cabbage lid, and tie string around the cabbage. Cook in salted water, about one hour. Serve with sauce made out of stock or melted butter.

FORCEMEAT

½ pound beef ⎫
½ pound pork ⎬—Grind together two or three times
½ pound veal ⎭
2 tablespoons flour
2 eggs
1 teaspoon salt
⅛ teaspoon pepper

Enough milk to make a soft mixture (about ½ cup)   EAC

Dinner Dish

Mold sausage meat into round patties and roll in bread crumbs. Place a slice of onion on top, then slice of tomato, a mound of cooked rice, and a mushroom cap. Bake in a moderate oven, 350° for 45 to 50 minutes.   MRS. LONGAKER

Saus

4 pigs feet
2 quarts water—add to maintain
Boil till soft—remove bones—cut fine
salt and pepper
  1 cup vinegar—dilute if desired less intense
  1 lemon—sliced thin
  1 envelope Knox gelatine

Combine ingredients and set in mold.   CUB

* Wheat flour is superior to white in dredging meat or fish.

Convent Pie

½ cup spaghetti (measure before cooking)
1 cup milk
¼ cup butter
1 cup soft bread crumbs
½ cup grated Italian cheese
3 eggs beaten
1 tablespoon chopped green peppers
1 tablespoon chopped parsley
1 teaspoon onion juice
1 teaspoon salt

Cook spaghetti and drain; scald milk, add cream and remaining ingredients. Bake in a greased baking dish in a pan of hot water for one hour. Serve with tomato sauce. MM

Meat Balls in Tomato Sauce

1 pound ground beef
1 onion grated or cut fine
celery cut fine, if desired
3 slices bread, soaked, or ½ cup bread crumbs
1 egg
salt, pepper and paprika to taste

Mix all together and form into small balls; roll in flour and drop into the following sauce and simmer slowly about ¾ hour.

1 can tomatoes
2 tablespoons catsup or chili sauce
1 tablespoon sugar JR

To Stuff a Round of Beef

Take suet, bread, pepper, salt, parsley, sweet marjoram, cloves, thyme, and the yolk of an egg minced fine, mix these ingredients with a little white wine. Then stuff the round. Tie it up and boil or bake it in a pot.

Fish and Spinach Casserole

2 pkgs. frozen spinach
2 pounds cod or other white fish
sharp cheese or ½ Swiss and ½ Parmesan according to desire for cheese flavor

In sauce pan put 1 carrot cut
1 celery cut
3 cloves garlic
parsley
2 cups water
} 5 minutes in pressure or till done in sauce pan

Wrap fish in old napkin and poach in this till done. 10 or 15 minutes. Lift fish out—remove any bones and put aside. Strain liquor and put in bottle to use as an excellent stock next day.

Cook spinach. Prepare light roux of it and butter and ½ tablespoons flour. Add this to puree of spinach. Cook till smooth and fine. Add some cream and as much beef essence as necessary.

Put spinach in greased baking dish. Now make a cream sauce with 2 tablespoons butter and 2 tablespoons flour, 1 cup milk, pinch sugar and paprika. Add the cheese and fish. Pour all on top of spinach. Sprinkly top with butter, a little more grated cheese and bake till golden brown in hot oven.

Seems like a lot of bother, but worth it.   MM

Virginia Sausage

20 pounds pork without bone—ground twice
   (13 pounds lean—7 fat)
3½ tablespoons salt
6 tablespoons fresh sage
2 tablespoons black pepper (fresh ground)

Put in sausage skins or leaf fat skins which have been scraped and placed in cold water to toughen. Then put in warm water when ready to use.   CUB

Beef Stew with Savory Dumplings

  1½   pounds boneless rump, cubed
  ¼   cup flour
  2   tablespoons bacon fat
  1½   quarts left-over vegetable water
  1   onion, sliced
  1½   teaspoons salt
  ½   teaspoon garlic salt
  ¼   teaspoon pepper
  3   large carrots
  3   large potatoes
  3   stalks of celery
  1   cup left-over cooked vegetables
        Dumpling batter

Dredge meat in flour. Heat fat in large Dutch oven, add meat and brown quickly. Cover meat with water saved from cooking vegetables. Add onion, garlic salt, salt and pepper. Cover and simmer slowly 1½ hours. Add cubed carrots, potatoes and celery, cut in one-inch pieces. Cook covered 25 minutes. Add left-over or canned vegetables such as corn and beans. Drop dumpling batter from teaspoon into top of stew to make 8 dumplings. Replace cover. Simmer 15 minutes. Serve at once.

Dumpling Batter

  2 cups sifted flour
  2 teaspoons baking powder
  1 tablespoon celery seed
     few sprigs parsley, minced
  1 teaspoon salt
  1 egg, well beaten
  3 tablespoons melted shortening
  ⅔ cup milk

Sift dry ingredients together. Add remaining ingredients. Mix only enough to moisten flour.   EH

Meat Loaf

    1   pound lean pork, ground
    1   pound veal
    2   eggs
    1¼ cups oatmeal
    Season with salt, pepper, and onion to taste
    1   can strained Campbell chicken noodle soup

Bake 2 hours, 325°   EAC

Meat Loaf a la Boop

    1 cup cracker crumbs   1 pound ground veal
    1 small can tomatoes   1 cup milk
    ½ green pepper cut fine   1 small can mushrooms
    1 teaspoon baking powder 1 teaspoon salt
    ½ teaspoon pepper   2 eggs, well beaten
    small garlic chopped fine   1 teaspoon sugar
    ½ pound ground pork   dash red pepper
    2 pounds ground beef

Mix and bake in slow oven about 1½ hours.   FBY

Meat Loaf

    1 pound of Happersett sausage meat
    2 pounds of hamburg
    2 eggs, cracker crumbs, onions, tomato soup or paste, celery

Fry four onions and outer stalks of celery slightly—not brown, just wilted—add sausage and hamburg, add eggs and ½ cup bread crumbs, salt and 3 tablespoons tomato paste and 1 or 2 teaspoons of Worcestershire sauce. Knead all together until mixed well—into loaf—roll loaf in cracker crumbs, place in roasting pan and cover with remaining tomato paste. Bake slowly 350° oven for one hour or one and one-half hours.

                                                                         EMT

Wheat flour is superior to white in dredging meat or fish.

Stuffed Meat Loaf

- 2 pounds beef, ground
- 4 slices bread, soaked in water and drained
- 1 onion, chopped fine
- 1 teaspoon salt
- 1/4 teaspoon pepper
- 2 eggs
- 1 recipe onion stuffing
- 3/4 cup chili sauce
- 1/4 cup water

Combine beef, bread, onion, salt, pepper and eggs. Mix thoroughly. Line bottom and sides of loaf pan with meat mixture. Fill center of pan with onion stuffing. Cover top with remaining meat. Spread chili sauce mixed with water over top and bake in moderate oven (350°) 45 minutes.

ONION STUFFING

- 3 onions, chopped fine
- 1/4 cup fat
- 3 cups soft bread crumbs
- 1 teaspoon sage
- 1 teaspoon thyme
- 1 teaspoon salt
- 2 tablespoons chopped parsley
- 3 tablespoons water
- 1 egg beaten

Cook onions slowly in melted fat until transparent, add bread crumbs, sage, salt, pepper and thyme and parsley and water. Sauté until slightly browned. Remove from fire and add beaten egg. Part chopped celery may be used instead of all onion, or the quantity of sage and thyme may be reduced if desired. EBT

Lamb Curry with Rice

Cut 2 onions fine

Put 2 tablespoons fat in pan and cook onions until yellow over low fire.

Add 2 tablespoons curry powder, and as soon as it is blended add 1 pound meat cut in squares as for stew. As soon as meat is seared, add 1 cup of tomatoes and cook over low fire for one to three hours. Add salt to taste.

When ready to serve, thicken juice with little flour and butter. Serve with dry rice and chutney. ABH

Sweet and Sour Spareribs

- 2 pounds spareribs, parboiled
- 1 cup pineapple, diced
- ½ cup mixed Chinese pickles
- 2 cups broth from spareribs
- 2 onions, minced
- 2 green peppers, minced
- 2 teaspoons cornstarch
- 2 teaspoons sugar
- 1 tablespoon soy bean sauce
- pepper and salt (very little)
- 1 tablespoon lemon juice

Mince onions and peppers and sauté in hot oil. Combine all ingredients and thicken gravy with cornstarch. Serve piping hot with rice.

Ham

Soak 24 hours, changing water twice. Cook slowly 3½ hours. Allow to cool in water in which it is cooked. For baking mix bread crumbs and brown sugar to roll it in and bake 2-3 hours slowly. Baste with wine.

RAISIN SAUCE

- 2 cups raisins
- 2 cups cold water
- ½ cup white sugar
- 2 scant tablespoons cornstarch
- ½ teaspoon cinnamon
- ⅛ teaspoon salt
- 3 teaspoons lemon juice or 1 tablespoon vinegar
- 1 tablespoon butter

Boil raisins in 1¾ cups water five minutes. Combine sugar, cornstarch, cinnamon and salt, moisten with remaining ¼ cup water, add to raisins stirring until mixture boils. Remove from fire, add butter and lemon juice; also if desired, stir in several stuffed olives, sliced thin, just before service.   MS

How to Bake a Ham

Cover the ham with cold water and let it simmer gently just long enough to loosen the skin, so that it can be pulled off. This will probably require from 2 to 3 hours, according to the size of the ham. When skinned, place in a dripping pan in the oven, pour over it a cupful of vinegar and one of hot water in which dissolve a teaspoonful of English mustard. Baste slowly, basting with the liquid every few minutes for 2 hours. Then cover the ham all over to the depth of 1 inch with brown sugar and do not baste again until the sugar has formed a thick crust, which it will soon do in a slow oven. Let it remain in a full hour after covering with sugar until it becomes a rich golden brown. When done drain from the liquor in the pan and put on a dish to cool. When cool, but not cold, press by turning a flat dish on top. The pressing makes it cut firmly. JJ

To Cure Hams

For each ham of about 15 pounds, put 1 ounce of salt petre, 1 gill of molasses, ½ ounce of pearl ash; put them in as much pickle as is requisite to cover the hams when closely packed. Let them remain in pickle for 6 or 7 weeks. The pickle should be strong enough to bear an egg. Have a small quantity of salt to keep it strong, after the hams are smoked they should have some hay applied on the fleshy part and inclosed in a bag or covering to exclude the flies. IPC

Ham Mousse

    1 cup grated ham
    1 cup whipped cream
    salt and cayenne pepper to taste

Stir all together. Pack in mould and freeze for 2 hours. ½ hour before serving take mould out and stand on top. This makes mousse soft and richer.

Calves Head—Turtle Fashion

Parboil the tongue, liver, lights and heart, save the water—then cut the head in square pieces, mix two good handfuls of onions and one of parsley chopped fine—sweet marjoram, thyme, black and cayenne pepper. Put a layer of the head, feet, etc., into the pot, then strew over it a handful of this seasoning till it is all put in, mix a lump of butter as big as a large onion with flour and put here and there in the pot. Pour over it the water that the head and feet were boiled in with a pint of wine and hang it over the fire—frequently shaking it to prevent its burning. Then wash the brains and pick them clean, mince about half a pound of lean veal with an equal quantity of suet or fat pork. Add two or three eggs, two biscuit finely powdered and about a third part of the seasoning above directed. Mix all well together and roll it with a little flour into balls and fry.

A Raggoo of Lamb

Set on a stewpan with some rich broth, (about 2 cups) put in some pepper and salt and half a dozen whole cloves; and add half dozen mushrooms, and a bunch of sweet herbs. Let these heat together. Then cut some lamb into moderately large pieces; beat them flat, and toss them up in a saucepan to brown them, and then put them into the broth, cover up the stewpan, and let them stew till they are enough. When the lamb is done, thicken up the sauce with some broth and serve it up hot.

Mutton, Venison Fashion

Let the butcher cut a leg of mutton, in the shape of a haunch of venison, and let it be a leg of a very fat and fine sheep; lay it with the back side downward in a deep pan, and gently pour on it a quart of red port wine; let it lie in this two days and nights, then roast it. Baste with some of the wine liquor of the pan and a little melted butter. When it is done, serve with nothing but its own gravy in the dish.

To Cure Beef and Pork

Pack the meat closely in the tub. Take 6 quarts of coarse salt, 1½ pounds brown sugar and 2 ounces salt petre. Put them in a pot with 5 gallons of water. Boil the whole over a slow fire together, scumming it all the while. When cold, pour it on the meat and the process is finished. The above quantity is sufficient for 200 pounds of meat or as much as the liquor will cover. It ought to lay 3 weeks in the pickle.

Beef Collops

Cut some beef steaks from the prime part of the rump, very nice, thin and small; let a stewpan be made perfectly clean, lay the steaks regularly in it, and grate some nutmeg over them; then put in an onion cut to pieces, a bunch of sweet herbs, some lemon peel cut small, a lump of butter rolled in flour, and about a quarter of a pint of rich gravy. Cover up the stewpan and set it over a gentle fire, let it stew some time, then make the fire brisker, and stir the whole together for some time as it simmers. When the steaks are near done, take out the bundle of sweet herbs, and add truffles, morels, mushrooms, and a little of the pickled mushroom liquor; when these are well heated together, pour the whole into a dish, strew on bread crumbs and brown nicely.

Beef Stroganoff

3 pounds of beef cut in 1" cubes
2 pounds fresh mushrooms
2 pounds onions
1 pint sour cream
1 cup tomato juice
1 cup tomato soup
1 tablespoon Worcestershire
dash of Tabasco
garlic if desired

Season and flour beef. Brown in iron skillet and place in Dutch Oven. Simmer until tender. Fry out onions and mushrooms together in butter and add to meat. Add all other ingredients. Simmer until ready to serve. Serve with fluffy rice. Serves 10 to 12 people.   EW

Beef Steaks in Ale

Beat some Rump Steaks to make them tender, then put into a stewpan half a pint of good mild ale; put the steaks in and let them fry. While they are doing cut an onion, and sprinkle over it some parsley and thyme shred small, grate on a little nutmeg and sprinkle over all some pepper and salt; mix all these together, and roll them up in a piece of butter, roll this in flour, and when the steaks are near enough, put it into the pan; shake all about that the butter may melt and the ingredients mix themselves in the sauce; then let them fry a few minutes more, and serve them up all together with the gravy, which will then be a very fine thickness.

Beef Steaks in Wine

Chuse some fine tender rump steaks, cut off the fat and set by itself; beat lean well, then put it into the pan with a very small piece of butter. Fry steaks over a gentle fire, often turning them, and pouring out the gravy as it runs from the meat. When the meat is enough fry the fat by itself, and thicken up the gravy that was poured from the meat in this manner; cut a shallot very fine, put it into the gravy, and sprinkle in some pepper and salt; grate in a little nutmeg, and add half an anchovy cut to pieces, and a gill of red port wine; boil this up together, with a piece of butter rolled in flour. Lay the fat upon the lean, and pour this gravy over them in the dish.

Swedish Pot Roast

    3 lb. Roast—allow 2 hours
    6 lb. Roast—allow 3 hours

Brown roast in butter or bacon fat. Salt and pepper to taste. Place in iron pot adding 3 cups boiling water. 1 onion sliced—4 whole allspice. Cook slowly until well done, thicken broth and add 2 tablespoons of sherry wine.

To Fry Sweetbreads

Squeeze into a small soup dish four fine lemons, take out the pips, and to the clear juice put some grated nutmeg, some pepper and salt, four whole cloves, and some chives cut small; stir all this together for a marinade. Blanch a couple of sweetbreads, and cut each of them, if large, into three or four pieces, if smaller only into two pieces; put these into the liquor, and let them lie in it an hour, frequently turning and stirring them about; then make a batter for them thus: beat up one egg with a little salt, mix it with some flour and water into a moderately thin condition, then melt about an ounce of butter and add to it; stir all together, and if too thick or too thin bring it to be right by a little flour or a little water. This being ready, take the sweetbreads out of the marinade and dry them in a napkin; when thoroughly dry dip them in the batter. Set on a stewpan with some hog lard, when it is hot take out the sweetbreads from the batter, and put them one by one into the pan; let them be fried perfectly brown, then take them up, and drain them carefully from the fat. Heat a dish, and lay over it a napkin also heated; lay the sweetbreads on this without any sauce, garnished with fried parsley. (The sweetbreads may also be rolled in flour and sautéed in butter, omitting the batter and deep fat.)

excellent VP

A Cheshire Pork Pie

Chuse a fine loin of pork, cut it into steaks, and take off the skin; pare a parcel of very good apples and having taken out the cores cut them into slices: These things being ready, make a good crust, and line a dish of a proper size with it; grate some nutmeg, mix with this some pepper and salt, and with this season the steaks well; lay in a layer of them first, then put over them a layer of apples, and sprinkle over these some powdered sugar, cover this with another layer of pork steaks seasoned as the first, and then pour in a pint of strong white wine; put in a little butter at top, then put on the crust, and bake carefully.

Sausage

    1 pound, fat and lean together, grind fine season with salt and pepper
    1 teaspoon sweet basil
    1 salt spoon each of marjoram and tarragon.

Mix well together and form into cakes   CPR

Bologna Sausage

Ten pounds of round of beef chopped very fine
2½ pounds of fresh pork cut in very small pieces with a knife
¼ ounce of mace and the same of cloves ground fine
2½ ounces of black pepper bruised in a mortar—not to be broken in more than 3 or 4 pieces each. Mix all well together and let it lay over night; then stuff it in the large skins of the beef, or lard skin will answer. Tie each sausage at each end with a strong string and lay them four or five days in the same pickle you make for hams. Then put them up to smoke. They are not fit for use till they are dried through.

Scrapple

Cook together for four hours one cleaned hog's head and 2 pounds of pig liver. Add 2 tablespoons salt. Meat must slip from bones easily. Remove bones and chop fairly fine. Do not grind as there should be small pieces of meat and liver. Season with sage, sweet basil and marjoram and return all to broth. The broth should be strong and flavorsome. Keep on low heat while adding slowly sufficient yellow corn meal and buckwheat in equal portions to make a soft mush, stirring constantly for the first 15 minutes and then frequently for ¾ of an hour. Use a large wooden spoon—if spoon will stand upright in pot of itself, enough meal has been added. Skim off greater part of fat. Pour into bread pans and keep in cool place. Slice like mush, dredge with thick coating of flour and fry till golden brown. Very nice served with poached eggs.   VP

Hamburgers

    1 pound hamburg   1 teaspoon grated onion
    1 teaspoon cornstarch   butter in pan size of walnut
    1 cup cream   pepper and salt

Put all ingredients (except butter and reserve ⅓ of the cream) in bowl and mix. Form small cakes quite round—put butter in frying pan—warm pan—put cakes in and turn until well cooked—about ½ hour—not too hot a fire. When cooked put on a platter and pour rest of cream in pan—add dash of kitchen bouquet and stir until well blended. Pour over cakes.

CPR

Hamburgers

Season ground meat with salt, pepper, a little cream and chopped onion. Roll into balls about 2 inches in diameter. Wrap strips of bacon around the balls and fasten with toothpicks. Broil or fry slowly on all sides. Serve with pan gravy.

VP

Veal Cutlet

Pound well with masher or hatchet. Score with sharp knife in diamond shapes. Soak in rich milk or cream three hours. Roll in fine bread crumbs and yolk of egg and cook as usual. Use milk for sauce.

Veal

Pound hard—soak in milk for 1½ hours before cooking. Turn veal occasionally in milk while soaking. Cook in double boiler—enough tomatoes cut up to fill a cup—sauté onion—add celery—put in double boiler. Put veal in iron skillet with plenty of butter and the vegetable mixture—cook slowly with cover at least an hour. Add the milk in which veal was soaked.

Lamb

Take French lamb chops and have all fat removed. Take mallet and mash till very thin. Just brown.   CPR

Rub baby lamb all over with garlic before cooking.

Ragout of Livers

Take one turkey's liver, and the livers of six chickens, pick the galls carefully away and throw the livers into cold water, set on a small saucepan with a quarter pint of strong gravy, put in the chicken livers, and then add two spoonfuls of pickled mushrooms and one spoonful of catchup; strew in a little pepper and salt, and, last of all, put in a small piece of butter rolled in flour. Let the whole stew together half a quarter of an hour and over a slow fire. In the meantime broil the turkey's liver. When all is ready, lay that in the middle of a small dish, take the chickens livers out of the saucepan and lay round it; then pour the sauce over all, and garnish with lemon. Frozen livers are easily obtainable.

MEMORANDA

MEMORANDA

MEMORANDA

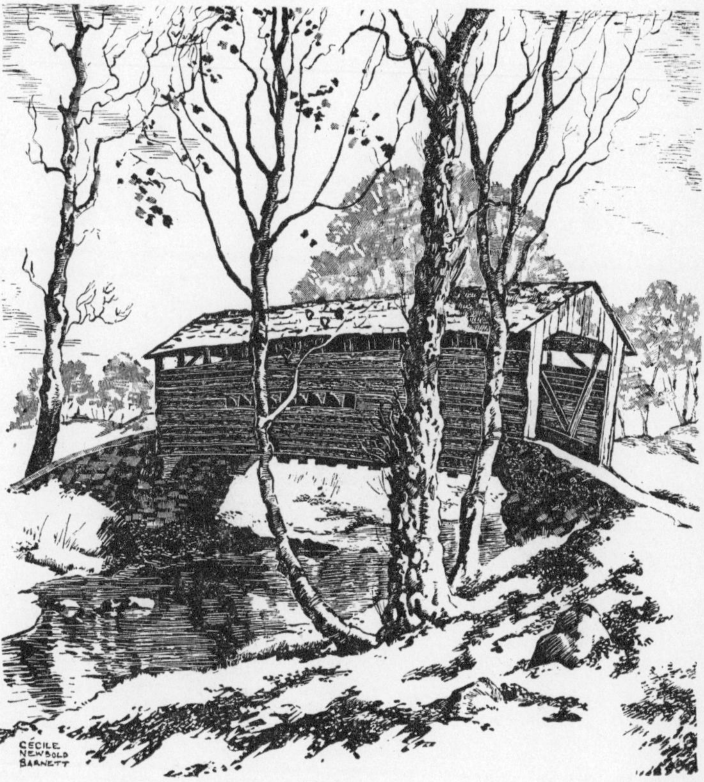
CÉCILE
NEWBOLD
BARNETT

SAUCES

Sauce for Venison

Claret, water and vinegar, each a glass
an onion stuck with cloves
an anchovy
salt and pepper. Boil and strain it. Serve it in a dish.

Newbury Sauce

Yolks of 8 hard boiled eggs—beaten absolutely smooth in one pint cream and ¼ pound butter.

Oyster Sauce

Open your oysters—save the liquor and put your oysters in water. Give them a whirl or two till they look white then put them in the liquor. Add flour and a large piece of butter, pepper, nutmeg and mace and wine. Shake them over the fire till quite hot but not let them boil.

Foamy Sauce

Three eggs, well beaten; two cups of pulverized sugar, one cup of cream, one half cup of sherry. Beat eggs to a cream, adding sugar gradually, also the cream whipped lightly, then the wine and beat all together. LBM

Raisin Sauce for Ham

¾ cup Raisins
1 cup water
4 or 5 cloves
¾ cup brown sugar
1 teaspoon cornstarch
¼ teaspoon salt
few grains pepper
1 tablespoon butter
1 tablespoon vinegar
¼ teaspoon Worcestershire

Cover the raisins with water, add cloves, simmer for 10 minutes. Add sugar, cornstarch, salt and pepper which have been mixed together. Stir until slightly thickened and add the remaining ingredients.

Cinnamon Sauce for Waffles (hot)

One-half cup of sugar, one-half cup of butter, one tablespoonful cinnamon (powdered), three tablespoonfuls of water. Mix sugar and cinnamon thoroughly. Boil water and butter, about three minutes with sugar and cinnamon. Just before serving add two tablespoonfuls of cream. LBM

Onion Sauce Plain

Chuse a quantity of large and sound onions, peel them, and put them into a great deal of water; set them on a clear fire, let them boil up; skim the water when anything rises; and when they have boiled three minutes pour them out into a sieve, and wash the saucepan, and put other water into it, put in the onions and let them boil two hours. Then drain them again, lay them upon a chopping board, chop them fine, and put them into a saucepan; drudge in a little flour, then put in a good piece of butter, and a good quantity of thick and rich cream; set the whole over a moderate fire to melt the butter and mix in the cream; and when all is well mingled it is enough. This is the common sauce for rabbits, and is very good for ducks; either must be boiled for this purpose; and when they are taken up and laid dry in the dish the sauce is to be poured over them. There must be a large quantity of it; smother them.

Gooseberry Sauce for Mackerel

Melt a little butter in a saucepan, add a dust of flour, brown it, and then throw in some chives minced very fine. When these have been heated together add some fish gravy, and throw in some bay, salt and a little pepper. Boil this up, then put in two or three sprigs of young fennel, and some small picked gooseberries; keep it simmering till the gooseberries are tender, and then serve it up together.

Sauce Robert

Cut some large onions into dice, or small square pieces, but not so small as by mincing, cut some fat bacon in the same manner, and put both together into a saucepan, set them over the fire, and keep them continually stirring about. When they begin to be brown pour off the fat, and pour in some rich veal gravy, add a little pepper and salt, and let them boil gently together till the onions are tender; then put in a little mustard and some vinegar, and serve it up hot. This is excellent with roast pork, and it eats very well with a roast goose and many other things.

Bouillon cubes or canned consomme can be substituted for veal gravy in many cases. The French prefer chicken broth.

Salad Dressing for Two

One cup of sour cream   one teaspoon sugar
half teaspoon vinegar   one small onion chopped fine

La Maise Sauce

1 tablespoon prepared mustard
1 pint mayonnaise   1 chopped hard cooked egg
1 pint chili sauce   1 teaspoon chopped chives
½ cup India relish   salt and pepper
       Serves 8—wonderful on shrimp   FR

Add 1 tablespoon honey to pint French dressing

Lemon Sauce

   1 heaping cup sugar
   ½ cup butter
   1 egg
Juice one lemon and a half rind grated.
   3 tablespoons boiling water

Beat white of egg, add yolk, beat again, then add sugar and butter. Beat well and put in lemon juice and water. Put on stove and bring to boil—do not boil—keep hot over boiling water. For puddings, cake, etc.

Cumberland Sauce

   3 tablespoons Red Currant Jelly
   1 glass Port Wine
Juice 2 oranges, the skins of the oranges cut in strips,
   1 pinch ginger
   1 blanched shallot, chopped very fine

Boil together for 10 minutes and serve cold.   CPR

Tartar Sauce

   ½ pint mayonnaise
   tablespoon chopped capers
   tablespoon chopped parsley   CPR

Cream Sauce

Melt over low heat 3 tablespoons of butter—add and blend in 1 tablespoon flour—stir in slowly ½ cup milk and ½ cup cream. Season with ¼ teaspoon salt and ⅛ teaspoon pepper. Cook and stir sauce with wire whisk until smooth and just about to boil. Use double boiler. This makes 1½ cups.

Take lump of butter and melt (not brown)—shake flour into butter and stir until fairly thick—add cream slowly stirring all the time—add salt and pepper.

Russian Dressing

   3 tablespoons Mayonnaise   chives cut fine
   1 tablespoon Chile sauce   dash of paprika
   1 teaspoon tarragon vinegar   dash of mustard
   1 chopped pimento   dash of salt

If too thick, thin with tarragon vinegar.

Hollandaise Sauce

   1 cup butter

Melt in saucepan but do not boil. Have double boiler ready with hot water in bottom (not boiling water). Take upper part and put yolks of four eggs and beat them thoroughly. Add hot melted butter (all off stove). If sauce seems thin put back on stove. If it looks like curdling add hot water. Keep beating all the time. Add salt and pepper, paprika and lemon juice to taste.   CPR

Hollandaise Sauce

   Yolks of 4 eggs
   4 tablespoons water
   8 oz. melted butter

Beat egg yolks and water over fire until fairly thick—thick enough to stick to whip. Add melted butter slowly—keep stirring—add salt and pepper to taste. Add 6 teaspoons of lemon juice. If it turns, add a bit of boiling water.

Use 1 quart copper saucepan and French whipper.   CPR

Hollandaise

    10 eggs
    1½ pounds butter
   lemon juice to taste

Melt butter, add slowly to the yolks of eggs in a double boiler with hot water in bottom, beating all the while.
Red or black pepper to taste
2 or 3 teaspoonfuls of hot water added.   CPR

MEMORANDA

MEMORANDA

MEMORANDA

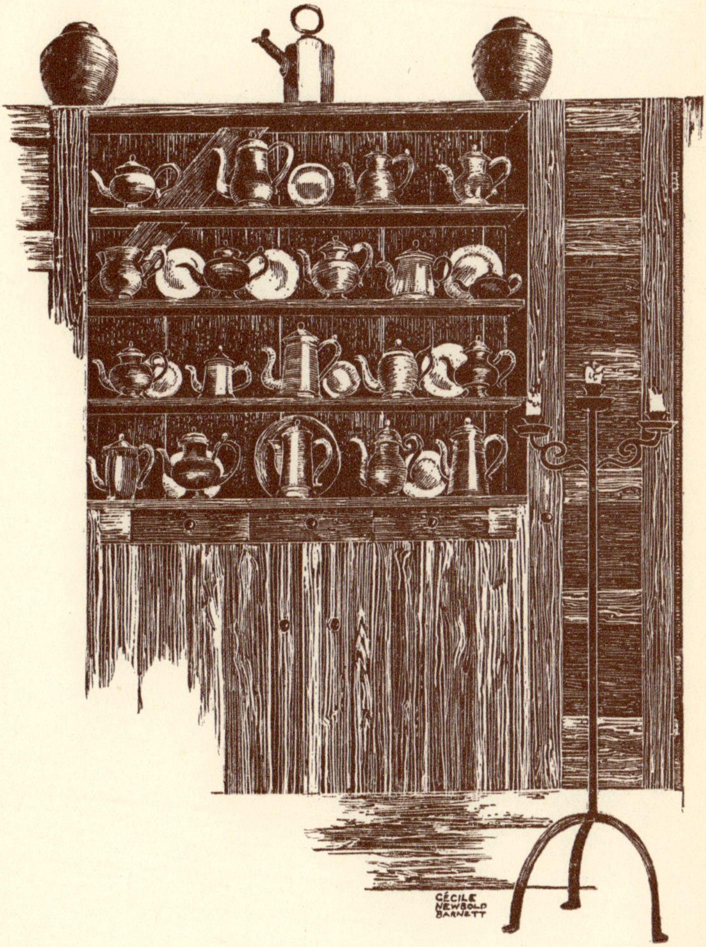
CÉCILE
NEWBOLD
BARNETT

GAME & FOWL

Fricasseed Rabbit

Skin and cut in pieces, lay in cold water a few minutes, drain and put in saucepan with pepper and one-quarter pound of pickled pork cut in strips, cover with water and let simmer one-half hour. Then add a small chopped onion, a tablespoonful of chopped parsley, a blade of mace and cloves. Mix to a smooth paste one tablespoonful of flour, stir it in, and let simmer till the meat is tender, then stir in one-half cup of rich cream; if not thick enough add a little more flour. Boil up once and serve. **LBM**

Wild Duck

RALEIGH HOTEL, WASHINGTON

The ducks are first roasted in a very hot oven (around 375 to 400°) for five minutes. They are then withdrawn from the oven and the breasts, in one piece, are carved from the carcass, without the wings—but with the legs. The skin is then removed and the carcasses are placed in a duck press from which the essence is extracted. The essence is then used as the basis for a sauce, to which is added ¼ pound of butter, some Worcestershire Sauce, six tablespoons of guava or currant jelly, salt and pepper to taste. This essence is heated in a flat pan or a chafing dish and the breasts of the ducks are cooked in same for not more than two or three minutes—or just sufficient time to brown them on the outside and rare in the center. The hearts and livers should be finely chopped up and cooked in another sauce consisting of three tablespoons of butter, salt and pepper, some chopped celery and carrots, some onions and approximately five ounces of sweet sherry. Then this sauce is then poured over the duck breasts (after they have been cooked sufficiently) and placed on a platter.

I assure you that wild duck cooked in this fashion is most delectable. RWW

Chicken

Split broiler—dot with butter, pepper and salt—dash of mustard. Start in oven in shallow pan, then put it on top of stove, cover and cook slowly for 2 hours at least. If necessary add more butter to baste at intervals. To test take fork and try to pull meat off of bone. Do not add stock or water.

White Fricassee

Take a fowl and cut it up. Put it into water enough to cover it. Stew it with a few grains of whole pepper and a sliced onion. When done take up and add to the liquor in which it was boiled, a little cream, flour, butter and salt worked together.

To Roast a Goose

As there is a distinction in the season of geese, according as they are young or full grown, so there is in the manner of dressing. For a full grown goose the method to be observed is this: prepare some seasoning for the belly thus: chop some sage and an onion fine, sprinkle over them some salt and pepper, and rolling all in a piece of butter, lay it ready to be put into the goose's belly. Let the goose be picked clean and wiped; or rather let it be managed thus: have about a gallon of river water scalding hot, dip the goose in it, and keep it under about two minutes, then take it out, pick it, and wipe it dry. The feathers will come off this way more easily and perfectly than any other and it takes off something from the great strength of the goose's taste. For such as love that high flavour this scalding may be omitted, and the onion may be left out of the seasoning when any person dislikes it; this must always be consulted according to the taste of those who are to eat it. Which ever way the goose is prepared, when it is clean picked, wiped, and dry, let the seasoning be put into the belly, and roast it. It must be basted with butter, and when half done a little flour is to be carefully dredged over it, and it is to be finished, frothed and brown. It should be served with two basons of sauce, one apples, the other gravy. A green goose need be roasted a little less and no seasoning should be put into it. These are often made flabby by too much scalding.

Chicken Croquettes

Half a good sized chicken. Chop fine. Chop fine one-half of onion, fry with one ounce of butter, add one-half tablespoonful of flour, stir for half a minute, then add the chopped meat, a little over a gill of broth, salt, pepper, pinch of nutmeg. Stir for about two minutes, take from fire, mix two yolks of eggs with it, put back, stir for one minute, add chopped mushrooms, or truffles or both together. Make bread crumbs of pastry crust, roll croquettes in shape, dip each one in beaten egg, roll in crumbs again and fry. LBM

Chicken Curry

Take a roasting chicken and cook until tender together with one can tomatoes, and a few carrots. When ready cooked, bone the chicken and have in large pieces. Then melt some butter and brown gently one large onion chopped, one tablespoon flour. Then add the stock from the chicken and few tablespoons of curry powder (more or less as desired). When cooked, strain and pour over the chicken and stir carefully so the pieces won't break. CPR

Chicken Curry

If chickens are young it is not necessary to parboil.
Put about 4 tablespoons butter, chicken fat or cooking oil in pan and brown gently three medium-sized onions chopped. Add the chicken cut in pieces for serving and brown slightly. Add 4 tablespoons flour and 2 tablespoons curry powder and stir well. Add one quart chicken broth or water and simmer about 1½ hours. The gravy should be slightly thick. Add salt and pepper and 1 dessert spoon of vinegar. Serve with boiled rice.

Wild rice is excellent. VP

Partridge

Lard them with slices of bacon, dredge and baste them. Lay them in pan, let them roast ten minutes. Take the grated crumbs of half a loaf of bread, put in a stew pan and shake lightly, until brown. Lay it between your birds and pour over them melted butter. Serve very hot. LBM

Quail

Take iron quail pot with top. Get it very hot. Put in some butter—lay the quail in—sprinkle them with pepper and salt—put top on and cook for 8 minutes, having turned them over once—Never touch any game with water—wipe thoroughly with paper napkins. CPR

Roasted Squabs

To boiled wild rice add a bit of finely chopped onion and minced mushrooms which have been sautéed in butter. Add salt, pepper, and celery seed. Stuff the squabs, sprinkle with salt and pepper and smear with fat and sprinkle with flour. Place in hot oven and roast, basting with the drippings in the pan and a little wine. Bake about 50 minutes. Do not overcook.

CPR

White Sauce for Turkey Hash

Use equal quantity of butter and flour. Melt butter but do not allow to sizzle, in a small saucepan over a low heat. When butter is melted add flour stirring well into the butter. Have some rich hot milk ready. When butter and flour mixture begin to bubble gently add the hot milk, very little at a time, stirring and beating well until the whole amount of milk has been added and the sauce is thick and creamy. Season lightly with salt and pepper. Add the beaten yolk of an egg after removing pan from fire and allow a little lemon juice.

CPR

Casserole of Duck with Sour Cream

Have a five or six pound duck cut up in convenient serving pieces. Dredge with flour and sauté well in fat. Place pieces in casserole and season with salt and pepper. Add the chopped giblets, one onion chopped fine, three tablespoons chopped parsley, a pinch of rosemary, one of thyme and a clove of garlic. Pour over this one cup of claret and cover tightly. Cook in moderate oven for two hours. Add a pint of sour cream and cook until tender. Serve with flaky rice.

Pigeons

When you have dressed your pigeons, roll a good lump of butter in chopped parsley with pepper and salt. Put it in your pigeons. Place in pan, dust and baste them. If a good fire, they will be done in twenty minutes. When ready, lay on hot dish and place around them bunches of asparagus with parsley and butter sauce.

MEMORANDA

MEMORANDA

MEMORANDA

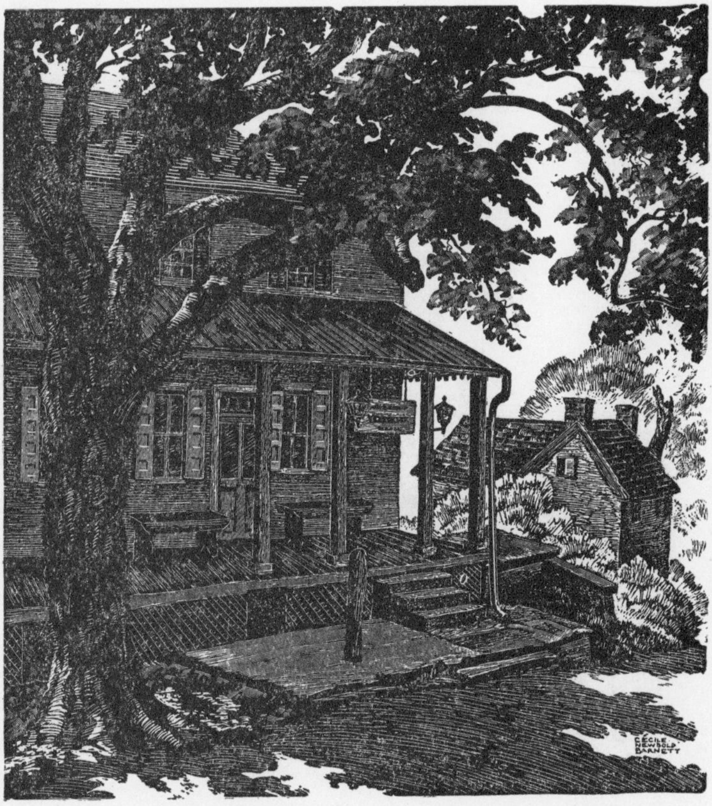
CECILE NEWBOLD BARNETT

EGGS & CHEESE

Welsh Rarebit

  1 pound cheese
  1 teaspoonful Worcestershire Sauce
  6 tablespoons musty ale
  1 salt spoon salt
  ½ teaspoon dry mustard
dash red pepper
  1 salt spoon white pepper
  2 yolks of egg—beaten and added just before serving
few drops onion juice

Use no butter

Put ale or beer in pan—cut up cheese and add ingredients.

A Welsh Rabbit

Cut a handsome piece of bread and an even slice of cheese, let the bread be of the shape of the cheese, but a little larger every way. Put a salamander in the fire, or a large poker, or the bottom of a fire shovel heated red hot will do. While the iron is heating toast the bread carefully on both sides, without making it hard or burning it. Then toast the cheese on one side, lay the bread in a plate, lay the cheese upon it with the toasted side downwards, hold the red hot iron over the other side to toast and brown that. Put a little mustard on it, and serve very hot, two together.

(The same effect can be attained with a broiler)

A Scotch Rabbit

Cut a slice of cheese very large and handsome, cut a slice of bread, without crust, just of the size of the cheese; toast the bread on both sides, and butter it, then toast the cheese on both sides, and let it evenly upon the toast and butter. Serve hot with mustard.

An English Rabbit

Cut a handsome loaf of bread without crust, and shave a good quantity of cheese very fine. Have in readiness a glass of red port wine. Toast the bread carefully on both sides, then pour the wine upon it, and turn it. When it has soaked up the wine spread the scraped cheese thick upon it, lay it in the oven, and place it near the broiler. The cheese will do very quickly and very finely. Serve hot. Superior.

These are the three ways of toasting cheese; the first is the genuine method, and those who are fond of cheese prefer it to either of the others. One would think nothing could be easier than to toast a slice of cheese, and yet not only in private families but at taverns we see nothing is done so badly. The directions here given are easy to be observed and they will never fail to be mellow, hot, well done and with the bread crisp and soft.

Stuffed Eggs Casserole

Hard boil two more eggs than the number of people you expect to serve. Shell, cut in two and stuff with any desired, rather spicy filling. Put a layer of eggs, small end down, in casserole, cover with ½ can of mushroom soup, thinned a little with cream. Add another layer of eggs, the rest of the can of soup and sprinkle with cracker or toast crumbs, put in medium oven till brown. This may be prepared the day before needed and kept in the ice box till just a few minutes before the meal. A good luncheon dish. FBY

Poached Eggs with Cucumbers

This is a very elegant little dish, and as it depends entirely upon the choice of each of the two articles, the eggs being new laid, and the cucumbers young and fresh, no time of the year can be properer for it than summer. Cut an onion to pieces, put it into a soup dish, pour upon it some vinegar, then add salt and pepper, stir all well together and cover it up. Get half a dozen young and fine cucumbers, peel them, split them open, and if there be large seeds in any, cut them out. When the cucumbers are thus prepared, put them into the soup dish to the vinegar and ingredients; let them be there an hour. Then take them out, put them into a saucepan, and toss them up with a piece of butter. When they begin to grow brown, pour in some broth, and set them over a gentle fire to simmer for a quarter of an hour. Choose half a dozen fine large and perfectly new laid eggs; break them into a cup one by one, and poach them in butter; lay them handsomely in a small dish one by one as they are done; cut away all the white so that nothing remains but the round yolk; and push these pretty close together. When they are all in, pour the raggoo of cucumbers over them hot, and serve immediately.

Shirred Eggs on Tomatoes

Cut a thin slice from the stem end of each tomato. Scoop out the pulp; slip in an egg, sprinkled with salt and pepper. Cover with buttered crumbs and bake until tomato and egg are tender and set. Cheese may be added also. EAC

Eggs Humpty-Dumpty

- 1 cup rich cream sauce
- 1 teaspoon tomato catsup
- 6 or 8 mushrooms, sautéed
- 3 hard-boiled eggs, sliced
- ½ cup grated American cheese

Add all together and heat until the cheese has melted. Serve upon very thin toast. MO

Scotch Eggs

    6 hard cooked eggs
    ½ cup, scant, grated bread crumbs
    1 cup milk
    1 cup finely chopped cooked ham
    ½ teaspoon mustard
    1 raw egg
   dash of cayenne

Combine milk and crumbs and heat stirring, till they make a paste. Stir in the ground ham, cayenne, mustard and slightly beaten raw egg. Mix well. Slice the hard cooked eggs and lay them in bottom of a buttered shallow fire proof dish. Cover with the ham mixture. Cover that with fine fresh bread crumbs (or an equal quantity of crumbs and grated cheese), set the dish in a pan with a little water and bake in a moderate oven until lightly touched with brown.   EG

Stuffed Eggs

   Pinch mustard
   Pinch salt
   1 drop vinegar
   butter to soften—mix well to egg yolks

Cheese Spread

Soften cream cheese with a little mayonnaise. Grate onion and cucumber and combine. Add salt and pepper to taste. May be served by dipping potato chips into the spread.   JR

Cheese Herbs

Sage	tarragon
Fennel seeds crushed	chervil
dill seeds crushed	dried chives

2 packages cream cheese, creamed. Top with ½ teaspoon herbs Spread on crackers or thin toast.   CPR

Cheese

The milk obtained from the cows at night we strain into the cheese tub and if the weather is so warm that there is danger of the milk turning sour before morning, we fill one or two tin pails full of cold water and sink them into the milk in the tub. This will keep the milk sweet. In the morning we take off the cream with a skimmer and put it in a vessel by itself. We then put the morning and night milk together; Then take one pailful of the milk and put it into a cauldron kettle, which is set in an arch for the purpose and start a slow fire till it is about blood heat. Then pour in the cream and stir it moderately till there are no particles of it to be seen floating on the surface; then dip milk enough from the tub to fill the kettle. Heat it so that when dipped back the whole will be about the same temperature as when it comes from the cow—then put in the rennet and stir it well, and then cover the tub with a cloth and let it remain till the milk is sufficiently coagulated, which, if the right quantity of rennet is used, will take from fifty minutes to an hour; then apply the curd breaker. Pour two or three dippers full of hot water on the curd, which will cause the whey and curd to separate; then dip off the whey in small quantities till you have obtained about twelve or fifteen quarts—heat this nearly to boiling, and dip it back into the tub, and stir it well with the hands; then dip out a kettle full of the whey, and while it is heating, break up the curd in the tub with the hands; as soon as the whey is near boiling pour it back into the tub and stir it and repeat this process till it is as hot as the hands can bear. By this time it is sufficiently scalded to whey off. We then spread a strainer in a sink, constructed with a rack in the bottom, made of narrow slats to allow the whey to run off. While the curd is cooling, keep working and breaking it. Curd cannot be made too fine for pressing. When it is nearly cool, salt it. To fifty pounds of curd, put three common size teacups of salt, and continue to work and break the curd till it is cool. Then put it into the hoop for pressing. Cheese cannot be pressed too hard—we press ours forty eight hours.

IPC—Hardinsburg, Penna

To Make Cream Cheese

Take five quarts of new milk and one quart of cream. Add as much boiling water as will make it milk warm. Then put to it a tablespoonful of good Rennet. Stir it together and let it stand till it comes, or curdles. Then lay a thin cloth in the cheese vat and put in the curd, breaking it as little as possible. Let the whey drain from it some time without pressing. Then cover it and put one pound weight upon it for an hour. Then lay on another pound. In three or four hours it must be turned into a clean cloth and four pounds weight put upon it. 24 hours will be long enough for it to remain in the vat. When taken out, sprinkle a little salt over both sides and lay it 2 or three days on a dry cloth turning it twice a day. Then lay it 3 days in fresh grape or rushes, changed every day. It will be fit to use in six days in warm weather.

To turn the curd for cheese cakes take 6 eggs to a quart of milk.

Cheese Pigs for Snacks

Cut the crusts off of slices of bread and cut slices into halves. The pieces will be about 1¼ x 3. Cut thin slices off Velveeta cheese and put between two pieces of this bread and wrap a slice of bacon around the sandwich and fasten with a toothpick. Broil slowly on all sides, watching carefully and they are finished when cheese is melted and bacon toasted. VP

MEMORANDA

MEMORANDA

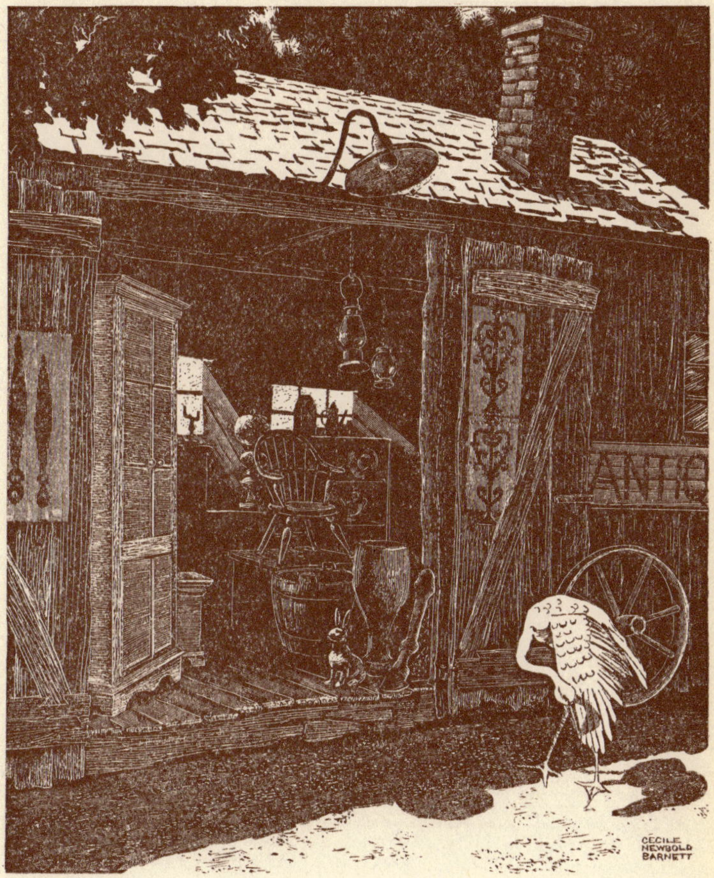
ANTIQ
CECILE
NEWBOLD
BARNETT

VEGETABLES

Baked Mashed Sweet Potatoes

1 pound of sweet potatoes—grated while hot
Add butter size of two eggs and the grated rind and juice of two lemons. Beat 1½ cups of granulated sugar and yolks of 3 eggs together. Stir in one cup of milk. Then add the well-beaten whites. Add salt to taste. Bake in greased baking dish.

Sweet Potato Pie

  1   pound sweet potatoes
butter size of an egg
rind of two lemons, grated. Also juice
  3   eggs
1½ cups granulated sugar
  1   cup of milk
  ½ cup brandy
  ½ teaspoon salt

Grate soft boiled potatoes—add one piece of butter—add grated rind of 2 lemons and add juice also. Take 3 egg yolks beat until light—add sifted sugar and milk and brandy. Then add beaten whites stiff enough to stand and a pinch of salt.

JD

To Boil Potatoes

This which seems very easy, is very often ill done; First see that the potatoes are sound and good, for many are bad. The red kind are better than the white but there is a yellow skinned sort that is best of all. Put them into the saucepan and then pour water to them; let it cover them an inch but not more. Most boiled things are spoiled by having too little water, but potatoes are commonly spoiled by too much. They must be perfectly covered, and a little allowed for waste in boiling, so that they may be covered at last; but the less does for this, because the water swells in heating. Let them be set upon the fire and the saucepan be close covered. Open it at times and look upon them; when they begin to crack they are enough. Drain the water clean from them, let them stand by three minutes; then peel them, lay them evenly in a plate, and pour over them thick melted butter. This may appear trifling to some persons, but some will thank us. VP

Creamed Potatoes

Bake and put in ice box still in jackets.
Next day peel and cut very small.
Season heavy cream with salt and pepper and just cover potatoes—simmer slowly ¾ hour to one hour. Add tiny bits of butter on top. Stir three times while cooking. CPR

Corn Souffle

1	tablespoon butter	1½	teaspoons salt
2	tablespoons flour	few grains pepper	
1	cup milk	2	eggs
1	quart corn		

Melt the butter, add the flour and gradually pour on the milk; bring to the boiling point, add corn, seasonings, yolks of eggs beaten until thick and lemon colored and whites of eggs beaten stiff and dry. Turn into a buttered dish and bake in a moderate oven from twenty five to thirty minutes.

Corn

Boil the ears, then with a knife score down the middle of each row of grains and scrape them off the cob with a fork; if done in this way most of the skins will be left on the cob. Then put the corn in a tin pan with butter, cream, pepper and salt. Place the pan in a kettle of boiling water, and stir in these ingredients until the butter is melted and all is mixed: this should be done just before serving.

Corn Fritters

Score and press one dozen ears of corn, and to every pint of pulp allow

- 2 eggs
- 2 heaping tablespoonfuls flour
- ½ teaspoon salt
- dash cayenne
- dash black pepper

Beat the eggs separately; add first the yolks and then the whites to the corn, mix gently, and add the salt, cayenne, pepper, and flour; mix again. Put two tablespoonfuls of lard or butter in a frying pan, when hot, drop the mixture by spoonfuls into it; when brown on one side, turn and brown on the other.

Serve very hot.

Creamed Corn and Beans

- 1 cup ground corn
- 1 cup fresh lima beans
- 3 eggs
- ⅛ teaspoon pepper
- 1 teaspoon salt
- 1 pint milk
- 2 tablespoons melted butter, fat or oil
- 1 teaspoon sugar

Mix the ingredients in the order given; pour into well-greased cups or ramekins, and steam until firm in center—about twenty-five minutes.

Corn Pudding

Young corn is not necessary—older less watery corn, freshly picked more desirable. Scrape with corn scorer, do not cut, from the cob, into shallow buttered baking dish. Add salt and pepper and dot generously with butter. Pour on about half cup of cream and top with small amount of brown sugar. (Omit sugar if corn is particularly sweet.) Bake in moderate oven until brown.   AHW

Corn Pudding

6	or 8 ears of corn, grated	2	eggs
1	tablespoon sugar	1½	pints milk
½	teaspoon salt	1	tablespoon butter.

Mix and bake 1 hour   Grandma H

Corn Oysters

2 ears of corn grated
1 pint of milk
2 eggs
1 teaspoon baking powder
1 tablespoon melted butter
Enough flour to make stiff batter
Drop by spoonfuls into hot fat.

Baked Mushrooms

Lay at the bottom of a small earthen dish a couple of slices of very fine bacon, minced, sprinkle over this some shred parsley, and strew on a little pepper; then lay in a good quantity of middle-sized mushrooms, well picked and skinned; sprinkle among these some pepper and salt; lay here and there among them a few shallots, then lay over them two or three more slices of bacon cut very thin, and strew upon this a blade of mace bruised to powder, and a little pepper. Cover closely and bake in a moderate oven till tender and brown.

Creamed Mushrooms

Skin and cut in half mushrooms, wash them off and place in double boiler with plenty of butter, allowing them to draw their own liquor, over low heat for two hours. Make paste of flour and butter and milk in accordance with amount of mushrooms, for a good creamy, dark and mellow consistency. Season to taste.

For a good cream sauce, use plenty of butter and always a double boiler.

Stewed Cucumbers

Pare a dozen of fine fresh gathered cucumbers; cut them into thick slices, and lay them on a coarse cloth to drain off some of the water. When they are pretty dry flour them, and fry them in fresh butter till they are of a fine brown; then take them out with an egg slice, and lay them in a plate before the fire, that they may keep warm. Pare another cucumber, and cut a slice lengthways out of it, that the seeds may be scooped out. Fill this with onions fried with the slices of the cucumbers just named. Strew a little pepper and salt over the fried onion before it is put in; then put the slice of the cucumber that was cut out into its place again, and tie it round with thread to keep it entire. Set this over the fire with some butter in a stewpan, and fry it till it be of a fine brown all over. Then take it out of the pan, lay it on a plate to keep warm also, and put in a little flour into the stewpan. Stir this carefully about, as it is dusted in; when the butter is well thickened, put in three spoonfuls of water; then add half a pint of white wine and two spoonfuls of ketchup. Stir all these well together, then put in three blades of mace, four whole cloves, half a nutmeg, and some pepper and salt. Stir all this well together, and pour it into a saucepan; put in the cucumbers, and toss them till they are all thoroughly hot, and relished with the sauce, then take out the whole cucumber carefully, and lay it in the middle of the dish, put this all round it, and pour the sauce over all; serve hot, garnished with fried onions.

Carrots with Sweet Marjoram

Boil carrots in small amount of water in tightly covered pan—add sweet marjoram and butter—let steam for 15 minutes—add 1 tablespoon of olive oil.

Carrot Souffle

Twelve medium carrots or 2 full cups. Cook well. Mash through ricer. Add 1 tablespoon grated onion, 1 tablespoon salt, 1 tablespoon sugar, ½ teaspoon white pepper and 1 teaspoon Worcestershire. Mix well. Add 3 eggs slightly beaten and 1 cup milk or mix carrot mixture to 4 eggs beaten separately, ½ cup bread crumbs and 1 cup heavy cream whipped. Put in ring mold and bake in pan of water about 45 minutes. Fill center with creamed chicken or other vegetable.

Cabbage

Wash and tear it in pieces and cut fine, and put it in a pot with boiling water which has already a pinch of soda. (Cut coarse stalks out). Boil ¾ hour. Put in collander and drain and press through the collander. Empty pot and put lump of butter and melt it, and replace cabbage and season with salt and pepper.   CPR

Red Cabbage

Slice red cabbage and soak in cold water. Heat a tablespoon of butter in saucepan, add cabbage and season with salt, pepper, nutmeg, one tablespoon sugar and some finely chopped onion and let the vegetable simmer for about 20 minutes or until it begins to cook a little dry. Then add two cupfuls of hot water and one or two peeled and finely sliced apples, a few cloves a tablespoon vinegar. Cover and let cook slowly until tender. One-third cup of currant or raspberry jelly adds greatly to this dish. Serve hot with mashed potatoes and goose.

Red Cabbage

    1 pound red cabbage   ½ cup sugar
    1 cup vinegar   salt to taste
    ½ cup butter   ½ glass tart jelly

Cut cabbage fine. Cook with vinegar, butter and salt until almost done. About one hour. Add sugar and jelly. Cook until done. Burns easily—watch it.   EAC

Real German Red Cabbage

    2 large heads of red cabbage
    1 large head of white cabbage

Slice thin into large bowl; sprinkle salt for every layer of cabbage—white cabbage added to balance strong flavor of red. Cut 1½ onions into very small pieces; cook over very low fire in 1½ tablespoon fat until thoroughly brown. Add 4 teaspoons paprika. Place shredded cabbage in large, covered kettle. Add one cup of water; boil until tender. Add onions and grease. Add one cup of sugar, and one cup of vinegar. Cook slowly for two hours.   CG

Cabbage with Rosemary

Boil shredded cabbage 20 minutes—½ cup water.
Add 1 tablespoon olive oil—3 sprigs of fresh rosemary and 1 teaspoon of dried rosemary.

Egg Plant—Turkish

    2 good sized egg plants, washed, peeled and chopped
    1 pound raw mutton (put through food chopper)

Season with salt, pepper, paprika, chopped onion, spray of parsley. Mix well and put in baking dish. Pour over this a rich tomato sauce and bake slowly. OR stuff egg-plant shells with mixture.

Fry sliced cucumbers in same way as egg plant.

Spinach

Wash spinach three or four times in warm water, cut off stems—put in pot and put lid on—cook five minutes—dash of soda—drain in sieve and save water. Put through meat grinder through smallest holes.

Put bacon fat in frying pan and let melt—try out grated onions—onions won't brown in bacon fat so add 1 tablespoon flour and cream—add spinach and water—salt and pepper—dash of allspice. CPR

Spinach Ring with Mushrooms

    ¼ peck spinach
    1 pound fresh mushrooms or 1 can
    2 tablespoons butter
    1 tablespoon flour
  salt and pepper

Wash, clean and boil the spinach as usual; drain and pack into ring mold which has been brushed with drippings; set in warm place until ready to serve. Turn out on hot chop plate and fill the center of the ring with mushrooms.

To prepare canned mushrooms: Drain the mushrooms and put into frying pan in which butter has been melted and sauté to a nice brown, then sprinkle with the flour and mix well; add the liquid from the can of mushrooms and enough milk or water to make one cup; cook three minutes. Season to taste. EG

French Artichokes

Cut the stems off even with the leaves—remove the hardest bottom leaves if there are any, and cut off the top ones straight across, leaving an opening, take out the inside or choke. Wash well, and place upside down to drain. Put them into boiling water for ½ hour or until the leaves pull out easily; drain well and serve on a napkin.

A Raggoo of Cauliflowers

All these raggoos of vegetables are to be made in the same general manner, but there are some little particularities to be observed in each on which the perfection and nicety of the dish depends; wherefore we have given these separate kinds as a direction for others.

Cauliflowers which are small, hard, and white are fit for raggooing, and the great art of the cook is to preserve their colour. This is to be done by first blanching them in white water in this manner. Set on a pot half full of very clear soft water, put in a slice of bacon and a piece of butter rolled in flour; stir this about as it heats, and it will be white, soft and thickish; as soon as it boils throw in three of these fine small cauliflowers, and let them boil till they are three parts done. Then take them up, set them to drain, and when the water is run off put them into a saucepan with some rich veal gravy, or some soup stock and let them simmer a while, then set the saucepan over a brisk fire, put in a piece of butter rolled in flour, and a teaspoonful of vinegar; when the butter is melted, and all well mixed, serve it up hot. The cauliflower no way eats so well.

Ragou of French Beans

Boil some young French beans till they are tender, then set them by to drain. Set a stewpan over the fire, throw in a piece of butter, let it melt, then drudge in a little flour, peel a large onion, cut it into thin slices, throw it in, and fry it till it is very brown. Beat up the yolk of an egg in half a cup of cream, let this stand by, put the drained French Beans into the stewpan, and grate in a little nutmeg; strew over them a little pepper and salt, and then shake them well about. When they are well mixed, and thoroughly hot, put in the egg and cream, and then shake them about over the fire two minutes. They will thus mix thoroughly together, and be well heated.

ATH

Poke Weed with Pennsylvania Dutch Dressing

Cook the poke until just tender and still bright green. (A pressure cooker is ideal for this—cook just one minute under pressure.) Poke is only good when the new shoots come up in the Spring. Don't separate the stalks but serve whole just like asparagus.

Serve hot with the following dressing:

Beat up one raw egg. Add a little salt, ½ cup vinegar, ½ cup water and a scant cup of sugar. Chip up two or three slices of bacon and try it out. When crisp, add to the other ingredients. Bring the whole mixture to a rolling boil, and pour hot over the cooked poke. Garnish the dish with chopped hard-boiled egg.

This same dressing may be used on young green dandelions, either raw or cooked. LPM

Green beans seasoned with 1 tablespoon currant jelly and 1 teaspoon prepared mustard. MM

Fried Tomatoes

Use ripe tomatoes—cut out stem and slice in two slices—roll in flour with salt and pepper added and saute slowly in butter, turning once, until nicely brown. Fire not too hot. Remove to large platter and to skillet add 1 tablespoon of flour, tablespoon brown sugar ½ cup thin cream. Stir until it boils, scraping all the brown loose. Pour over fried tomatoes. If some of the tomatoes have broken up and mashed or stuck to skillet, it adds delightfully to the gravy. VP

Apples

Slice apples—put in frying pan with ½ water and ½ bacon fat till slightly soft. Drain and put in baking dish—add butter and sugar—finish cooking in oven. CPR

Glazed Onions

Cook 3 cups small skinned silver onions in boiling salted water for 15 minutes. Drain and dry on cheese cloth. Melt 3 tablespoons of butter, add 2 tablespoons of sugar and the onions. Cook 20 minutes, or until browned—using an asbestos pad.

JD

MEMORANDA

MEMORANDA

MEMORANDA

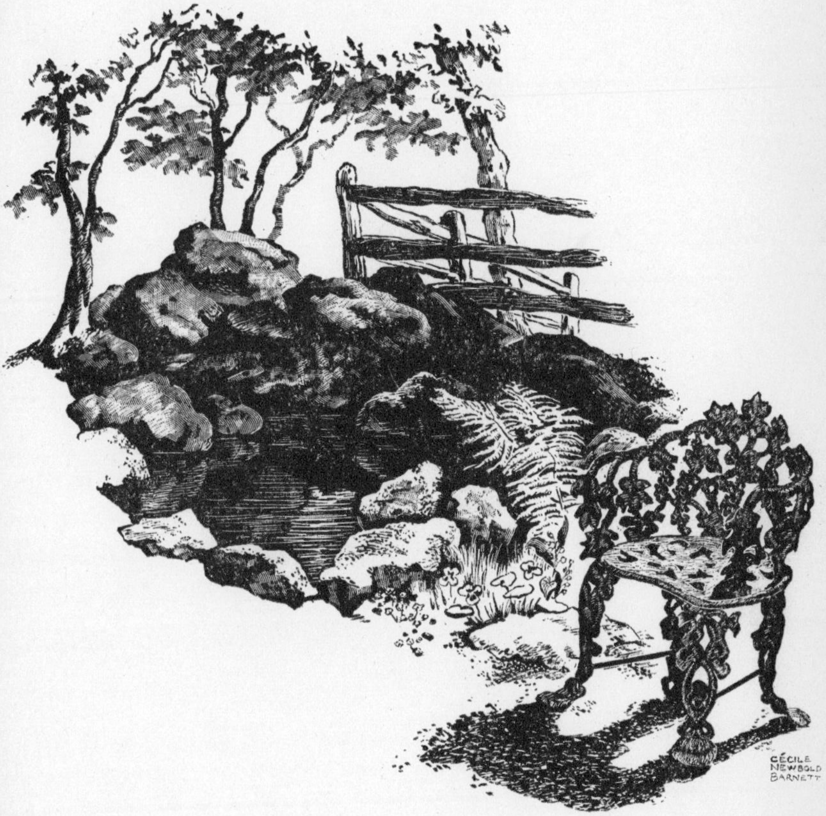
CÉCILE
NEWBOLD
BARNETT

SALADS

Heavenly Salad

    1 can sliced pineapple
    1 pound white grapes or 1 can cherries or both
    ½ pound marshmallows

Cut fruit and drain, add marshmallows cut in fine pieces

    Dressing: juice of 1 lemon
    2 egg yolks,   ½ teaspoon mustard

Cook thick, when cool add ½ pint of whipped cream. Then mix into fruit and marshmallows. Let stand all day on ice or make the day before. Serve on lettuce with maraschino cherries on top. Nuts may also be used. Will serve 10.   KMW

Broccoli Salad

Cook 1 large head of broccoli, or 2 packages of frozen. Use the upper portion only for the salad. Hard cook 6 eggs and chop fine. Add the cooked broccoli and ¾ cup mayonnaise to the eggs. Soften 1 envelope unflavored gelatin in ¼ cup canned condensed consomme. Heat the rest of the consomme and dissolve the softened gelatin in it. Cool. Add the egg and broccoli mixture. Season with 1-¾ teaspoons salt, 2 teaspoons lemon juice, ¼ teaspoon Worcestershire sauce, a dash of Tabasco. Turn into a mold. Chill until firm. Serve on lettuce leaves with mayonnaise. This salad is best made the day before, but it will set in rapid-freezing compartment in 1 hour. Crab meat may be substituted for broccoli.   BYL

Jellied Vegetable Salad

    1 package lemon flavored gelatin
    1 cup hot water
    1 cup tomato juice
    1 tablespoon lemon juice
    ¼ teaspoon salt
    2 cups shredded cabbage
    1 medium size cucumber
    2 scallions, sliced very thin

Pour the boiling hot water over the lemon flavored gelatin and stir until dissolved. Then add the tomato juice and set aside to cool. When the mixture begins to stiffen, add shredded cabbage, cucumber, sliced scallions, lemon juice and salt. Pour into a mold and put into the refrigerator until firm. Turn out on lettuce or greens and serve.

To make horseradish mayonnaise, mix thoroughly ½ cup mayonnaise and 1 teaspoon grated horseradish.   EG

Fruit Salad or Dessert

    2½ cups graham cracker crumbs
    1 medium sized can crushed pineapple (1 cup)
    1 cup chopped English walnuts (½ pound)
    1 tablespoon cream
    1 egg
    ¼ teaspoon salt
    1 cup sugar
    ½ cup butter

Cream butter and sugar thoroughly. Beat egg yolks slightly, and thoroughly beat into sugar mixture. Beat in cream and stir in the thoroughly drained pineapple. Beat egg white and fold into mixture. Add salt. Line a deep oblong pan with heavy waxed paper both bottom and sides. Put in one inch layer of graham cracker crumbs and sprinkle with 3 tablespoons of the juice from the pineapple and cover with ⅓ of the pineapple mixture. Sprinkle ⅓ of the nuts over this. Repeat so that you have 3 layers of each in the same order. Cover with waxed paper and let stand over night in the refrigerator. Serve cut-down in slices with whipped cream. (½ pint of whipping cream.)

Mother's Fruit Salad

Dressing: Drain juice from 1 large can pineapple. Add 1 tablespoon butter and heat. Mix ½ cup sugar and 1 tablespoon flour and add to the juice. Then add 2 eggs well beaten. Cook very slowly to avoid burning. Cool and add ½ pint cream whipped.

    Cut up 8 slices pineapple, or pineapple wedges
    3 bananas
    ¼ pound marshmallows

Combine with dressing and add nutmeats if desired. Serves 12.

JR

Prune Salad Mold

1 package orange gelatin	¼ teaspoon salt
1 cup boiling prune juice	½ cup diced celery
½ cup orange juice	⅓ cup broken nuts
2 tablespoons lemon juice	1 cup cottage cheese
1 cup cooked, seeded prunes	

Dissolve gelatin in prune juice, add orange and lemon juices, cool until slightly thick. Mix in prunes, salt, celery, and nuts. Chill until quite thick and pour over cheese in bottom of mold, rinsed out of cold water. Chill. Unmold on crisp lettuce.

MS

Raisin Sunflower Salad

¼ pint cottage cheese	peaches, fresh or canned
mayonnaise	½ cup Sun-Maid seedless raisins
salt	lettuce

Make a smooth paste of the cheese and mayonnaise; salt to taste. Arrange slices of fruit on center of lettuce leaf to resemble petals of sunflower; place cottage cheese in mound over center section of slices. On top of cheese arrange raisins to resemble sunflower seeds. Bananas sliced thin may be substituted for the cheese. Serve with mayonnaise and juice of peaches mixed.

EG

Cole Slaw

    1 quart of cut cabbage   1 teaspoon salt
    ½ cup of cream (sour is best)   pepper
    2 tablespoons vinegar   butter size of walnut
    2 eggs

Cut cabbage very fine and put in earthen bowl. Put vinegar on to boil. Beat the eggs until light, add the cream and butter. Now add these to the boiling vinegar and stir until boiling hot. Add the salt and pepper and pour over the cabbage. It is now ready to serve when very cold.   CPR

Cole Slaw Dressing

    ¾ tumbler of white vinegar   ¼ teaspoons dry mustard
    ¼ tumbler water   2 eggs beaten
    4 teaspoons sugar

Mix in order given and cook slowly till mixture thickens, stirring constantly.   CM

Salad

Salad greens with hard boiled eggs, tarragon, raw herbs as well as the tarragon vinegar. A whole leek well cut up and slight touch of onion and mustard.

Salad

    1 head endive—chop in ½ inch lengths
    1 head chickory—chop
    1 head lettuce—chop
    1 bunch water cress—chop
    celery with heads—chopped
    beet and tomato—cut up

French dressing. Stir part of beaten raw egg in—very cold—about 2 teaspoonfuls. Mix thoroughly—turn over and over—put hard boiled egg through colander and garnish with it.

    CPR

Chicken Salad Californian

   1   Avocado
1 ½   cups diced cooked chicken
   1   cup diced celery
   1   small diced hard head of lettuce
   ¼   cup chopped pimento
   2   tablespoons chopped green onion
   ½   teaspoon salt
   ⅓   cup of mayonnaise
   1   tablespoon lemon juice
lettuce for garnish (or watercress)

Cut Avocado in half. Remove seed and strip off skin. Cut the pulp into dice. The day before using, remove core from lettuce. Let cold water run into cavity with full force for a minute. Shake well to drain off all possible water. Wrap in a towel and put in refrigerator to get dry and crisp. When you arrange the salad, cut the lettuce in slices just before using. Cut the slices into cubes. Dice the chicken and season it with a little pepper. Mix the lemon juice with the mayonnaise. Then combine all ingredients and toss lightly to mix. Serve with crisp little lettuce leaves or water cress garnishing the salad bowl.

EG

Lettuce with Sour Cream Dressing

Put enough lettuce for one meal in bowl, then add about ¾ cup heavy sour or sweet cream, dash salt, sugar and vinegar to taste, then stir with large fork until foamy, add a little more cream, sugar and vinegar if necessary.

Supreme Salad

   1 cup grated carrots
   1 cup chopped celery
   1 package lemon jello ⎫
   1 cup hot water   ⎬ let cool
   1 cup crushed pineapple ⎭

Serve on lettuce leaves.

Boiled Deutch Salad Dressing

    3 slices or more of bacon   2 tablespoons of sugar
    1 cup of vinegar   ½ teaspoon salt
    2 eggs

Cut bacon in small pieces; fry in a skillet till golden brown. Mix eggs, sugar, salt with vinegar in a bowl. If vinegar is very strong mix one half vinegar and the other half water. Pour this mixture into the bacon, let it come to a boil; turn off and pour over your salads or vegetables.   LT

Pear-Lime Salad

1 package Lime Jello dissolved in 1 cup hot water. Add 1 cup juice from canned pears. Pour about ¼ inch deep in bread pan and leave remainder in bowl. Chill both. Let that in bread pan harden, and that in bowl just so it can be whipped. Dice drained pears. Soften 2 packages Philadelphia Cream Cheese by adding a little of the whipped Jello. Combine the pears, cream cheese, whipped Jello and a pinch of ground ginger, and pour into the pan over the plain Jello which should be set firm. Chill again and unmold when ready to serve. May be served on lettuce with mayonnaise.   JR

Cucumber Aspic

    3 or 4 cucumbers
    2 small onions
    1 box lemon Jello
    2 cups boiling water to which has been added
    1 tablespoon vinegar
    red and black pepper to taste

Peel and dice cucumbers and onions, chill them in ice water. Pour the boiling water over jello, and when this mixture begins to thicken, add cucumbers and onions, then put in favorite mold to jell.   MCE

Southern Salad

Take tender okras, trim the ends, boil till tender, drain and let become very cold. Dip some peppers in hot fat and take off the skins, then finely shred them like matches, mix them with okras, and serve with desired dressing. LBM

Nectar Dressing for Fruit Salad

  1 Philadelphia Cream Cheese ⎫ cream together
  2 tablespoons honey ⎭
Grated rind of lemon
  2 teaspoons lemon juice
salt
¾ cup oil added few drops at a time.

Nectar Dressing No. 2

  ⅓ cup mayonnaise   ⅓ cup cream
  ⅓ cup honey   whip together   VP

MEMORANDA

MEMORANDA

MEMORANDA

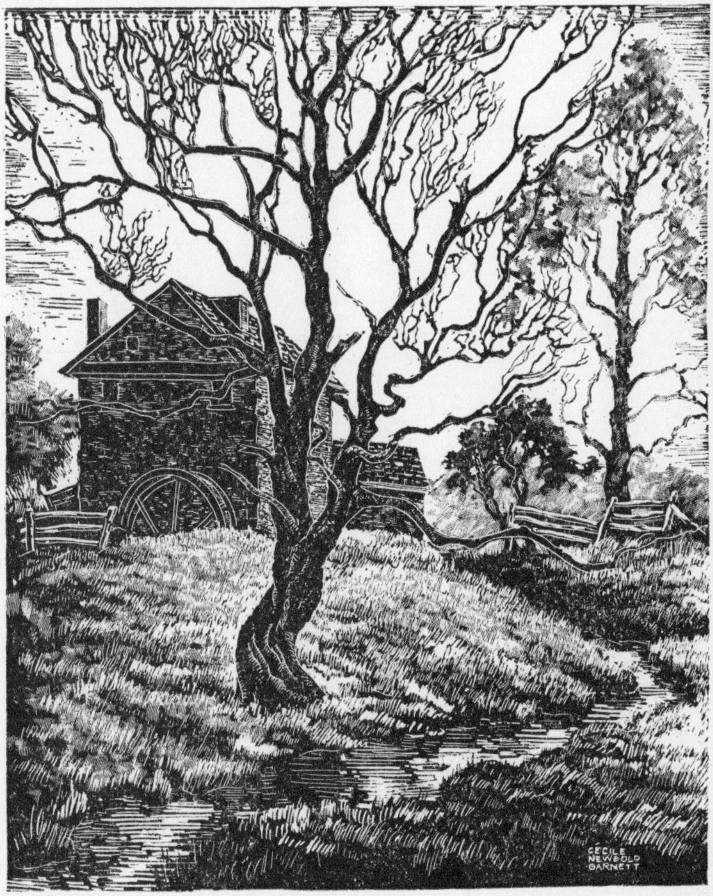
CECILE
NEWBOLD
GARNETT

BREADS

Bread Mixture

    3 tablespoons butter   4 cups flour, sifted
    1 cup sugar   4 teaspoons baking powder
    3 eggs   1 teaspoon salt
    ¾ cup milk   orange mixture

Mix in order given and bake in loaf pans.   JR

Southern Spoon Bread

    ½ cup sifted corn meal (white)
    1 tablespoon butter
    ½ cup sweet milk
    1 cup boiling water
    ½ teaspoon salt
    1 egg
    1 tablespoon baking powder

Pour water over meal, stir till smooth and cook briskly 5 minutes. Add butter and salt, stirring while it cooks. Take from fire, add milk, beaten egg and baking powder. Pour into buttered shallow pan and bake 20 minutes in moderate oven.   VP

Brown Bread

    1 cup each: corn meal, rye flour, whole wheat flour
    1 cup molasses
    1 cup water
    1 teaspoonful soda—salt, raisins may be added

Steam in buttered tin 3½ hours

Note: for family of two, make half the recipe   ENT

Orange Bread

    Rinds of 4 or 5 oranges (juice may be used for other purposes)
    Wash. Boil in salted water for 10 minutes
    Drain. Scoop out loose membrane
    Run through food chopper

Make a syrup of 1½ cups sugar and ¾ cup water
Boil orange rind in syrup until quite thick, stirring occasionally.
Cool. (This orange mixture may be prepared in advance and kept in refrigerator until ready for baking bread.)

Steamed Corn Bread

¾	cup flour	½	teaspoon salt
2	cups corn meal	2	eggs
4	teaspoons baking powder	1½	cups milk
		5	tablespoons melted butter
3	tablespoons sugar		

Sift the dry ingredients, add corn meal, beat eggs well, add sugar. Add the dry ingredients and liquids alternately. Add melted butter and stir well.

Place in well-greased steamer or coffee can. Put one cup of water in the cooker. Place corn bread on trivet. Turn switch to high. When steam escapes from vent, turn switch to medium. Entire cooking period, two hours.   MRS. L

Rice Bread

  3   teacups of boiled rice
  1   teacup wheat flour
  1½ pints of milk
  2   ounces of butter
  5   eggs beat separately
Indian meal to make a batter as thick as pound cake.

Bake in soup plates ¾ of an hour.   IRC

Christmas Bread

  2   packs yeast
  ¼ cup lukewarm water   } let stand 5 minutes
  ¼ teaspoon sugar

  1   pint milk—scald and cool to lukewarm

  1   cup butter
  1   cup sugar
  1½ teaspoons salt
  2   eggs—well beaten   } cream together
  ½ teaspoon cardamon
  ½ teaspoon clove
  ½ teaspoon nutmeg
  1   teaspoon cinnamon

  7   cups or more of flour
  1   cup raisins
  1   cup nuts broken in pieces   } dusted with flour
  1   cup mixed candied fruit

Add yeast to milk—beat in 3 cups of the flour till smooth. Add creamed mixture and four more cups of flour—mix till a smooth soft dough. Mix in raisins, nuts and fruit—work in with hands or rolling pin (quite a job). Let rise in warm place till double in bulk. Form into 3 equal loaves. Let rise till double in bulk—brush tops with mixture of beaten-egg yolk and ¼ cup milk. Bake one hour at 350°.   KT

Muffins

- 1 cup cold oatmeal
- 1½ cups flour—1 teaspoon sugar
- 1 beaten egg—salt
- 4 teaspoons baking powder

Mix into stiff batter with milk   EH

Corn Meal Muffins

- 2 cups of white corn meal
- 2 tablespoons butter
- 1 teaspoon salt
- 1 teaspoon baking powder
- 2 eggs
- 1½ cups boiling water
- ½ cup milk

Put corn meal, butter and salt in a bowl and pour over this the boiling water—which must be boiling hot—and mix thoroughly. While this is cooling, beat the eggs without separating until very light—add with the milk and baking powder to the corn meal. Then bake in a well-buttered muffin pan for 20 or 25 minutes in a very hot oven.

Crullers

- 2 pounds flour
- rather more than ½ pound of sugar
- ½ pound butter
- 6 eggs
- ½ glass brandy—same of rose water
- ½ a nutmeg

Beat your butter to a cream—the eggs to a froth—roll it out cut in what form you please—boil them in lard.

Popovers

One cup of milk, one cup of flour, two eggs, one-half teaspoonful of salt. Bake thirty to forty minutes in moderate oven in small brown bowls half full.   LBM

Buns

- 1¼ pounds flour
- ¾ pound sugar
- ½ pound butter
- 6 eggs
- 1 wine glass of brandy
- ½ nutmeg
- 1 handful of currants
- ½ pint of new milk
- ½ teacup yeast

Mix and let stand over night.

Quick Cinnamon Buns

One cup of sugar, one tablespoonful of butter, two cups of flour, two teaspoonfuls of baking powder, a pinch of salt. Spread out in shallow pan and dot butter over it. Sprinkle with cinnamon and brown sugar and currants or muscatel raisins pressed in. Bake in moderate oven. LBM

Potato Buns

- 1 cup mashed potatoes
- 1 cup sugar
- 1 yeast cake dissolved in 1 cup luke-warm water
- ½ cup melted butter
- 3 eggs well beaten

Gold Medal flour to make a light bread dough.

Let rise 3 or 4 hours or until double its size, then roll out about ½ inch thick and cut with a cookie cutter and place on a baking sheet and let rise till twice their size; then bake in moderate oven. I make 20 dozen at a time and freeze them after they are baked. Put them frozen into a slow oven for 20 minutes. They are just like fresh baked buns. This recipe makes about 5 dozen small buns or 3 dozen large ones. MRS. MB

Waffles

- 1 pound of flour
- ½ pound butter
- 4 eggs
- 1 quart of milk
- yeast

IPC

Waffles

    large teaspoon of soda
    1 quart buttermilk
    3 eggs—separated
    pinch salt
    half cup butter—melted
    enough batter flour to make little thicker than flannel cake batter
    Add beaten egg whites last.   CPR—1914

Waffles

    1 pint milk   salt
    enough flour to make a batter   yolks of 3 eggs
    piece of butter size of walnut   ½ cup yeast

Let rise for 6 hours. Then beat in the whites of 3 eggs and bake at once in waffle irons.   CPR

Short Bread Biscuits

    ¾ pound flour   4 ounces sugar
    ½ pound rice flour   ½ pound butter

Beat butter and sugar to a cream. Add flour and rice flour. Work to a smooth paste. Roll out and cut in rounds quarter inch thick. Bake in medium oven.

Sour Milk Biscuit (100 years old)

    1 quart flour
    1 teaspoon salt
    2 heaping teaspoons cream tartar
    2 teaspoons soda
    4 rounded tablespoons shortening
    Sour milk or buttermilk to mix, not too dry. Hot oven.

    EH

Rusk

   2 pints flour
   2 teacups sugar
a piece of butter the size of a goose egg
   2 teaspoonfuls cream of tartar
⅔ of a teaspoonful soda
milk enough to make a soft dough

MEMORANDA

MEMORANDA

MEMORANDA

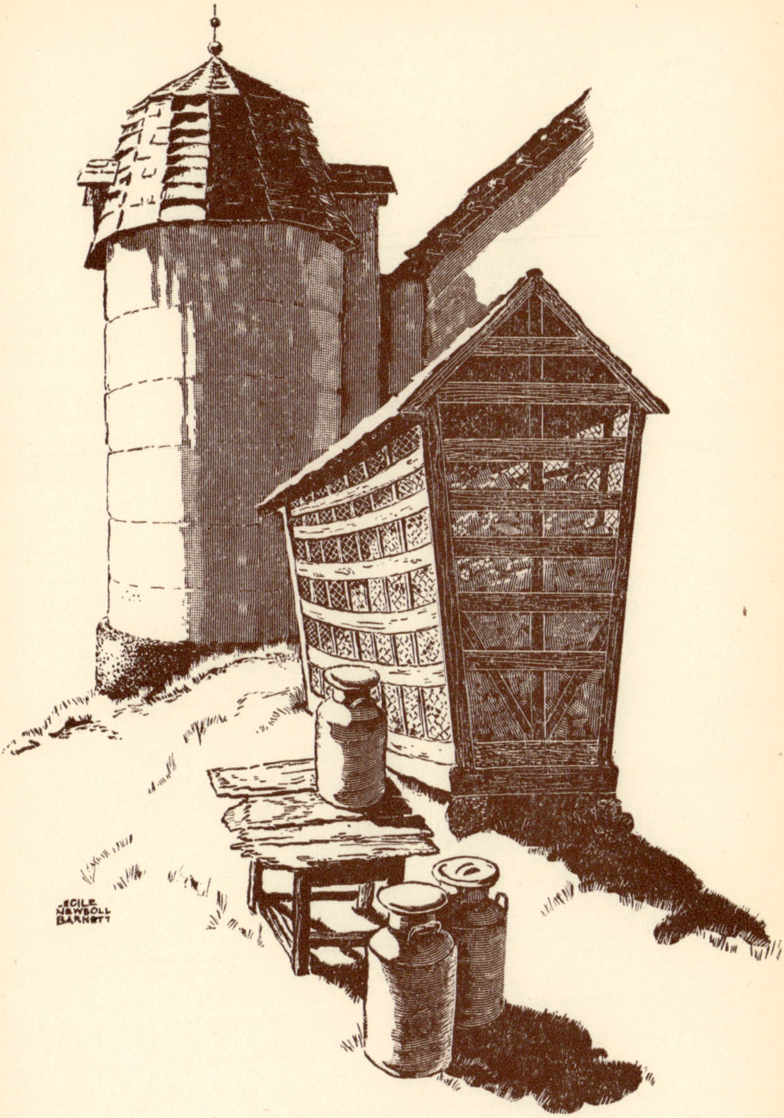
CECILE
NEWBOLL
BARNETT

CAKES

Lemon Cake

    2½ cups sugar   4 eggs
    ¾ cup butter   3½ cups flour
    1 cup cream

Two and one-half cups of sugar, three-fourths cup of butter, three and one-half cups of flour well sifted, one cup of cream or milk, four eggs, rind of one lemon, juice of one and one-half lemons, one teaspoonful of baking soda dissolved in milk. Rub butter, sugar, yolks and rind very well together, until sugar is dissolved. Then add one-half the milk and one-half the flour and remainder of both, and then the whites and lastly the lemon juice. This will make three cakes in medium sized pans.

LEMON JELLY

Two cups of sugar, yolks of three eggs, juice of two lemons. Cook until thickened in a double boiler. Then add the well beaten whites of the eggs. Put between layers of cake.   LBM

Lady Cake

    2   cups sugar   ½ cup cornstarch
    1   cup milk   whites of four eggs—fold in last
    ½   cup butter   2   teaspoons baking powder
    2½   cups flour   bitter almond flavoring   ST

Plum Cake

    1   pound of butter beat to a cream
    1   pound of sugar
    12   eggs well beat
    1¼   pounds flour
    2   pounds currants—1 of raisins
    ¾   pound citron and a large wine glass of brandy
ground cloves

Hot oven.   CPR

Blueberry Cake

    1   cup sugar   1 quart flour—salt
    ½   cup shortening   1 teaspoon soda
    2   eggs   1 quart blueberries added last
    1   pint milk   EH

Feather Cake

    4 eggs
    2 cups sugar
    1 cup butter or other shortening
    1 cup sweet milk
    3 cups flour
    2 teaspoons baking powder
    1 teaspoon vanilla
    pinch of salt

Cream sugar and shortening—add egg yolks and salt. Add milk and flour and vanilla. Add beaten egg whites last.

Bake in layer cake pans—makes four layers.   MRS. CRH

Boiled Raisin Cake

1 package raisins cooked until swelled up—in enough water to make 2 cups of juice. Let cool before using.

3 cups sugar	1 tablespoon cocoa
1 cup shortening	½ teaspoon cloves
1 cup walnut meats	½ teaspoon nutmeg
4 cups flour	½ teaspoon cinnamon
1 egg	2 scant teaspoons soda

Cream shortening and sugar. Add beaten eggs.
Mix the soda with boiled raisins and add. Add the cocoa and spices to the flour and combine. Last, add the chopped nuts. Makes 1 large or two small cakes. Bake at least an hour 350°, or until nicely brown on all sides. If small pans are used, not necessary to bake so long. EAC

Chocolate Spice Cakes

Sift some flour, measure 2 cups full, add ½ teaspoon of soda, ½ teaspoon of salt, 1 teaspoon of cinnamon, ¾ teaspoon of nutmeg and 3 tablespoons of cocoa and sift again two times.

Beat ¾ cup of shortening and gradually beat ¾ cup of sugar into them. Then combine the two sugar mixtures, add 1 teaspoon of vanilla and beat until grain of sugar is smooth.

Measure ¾ cup of sour milk or buttermilk. Or if neither of these is at hand, use ¾ cup of sweet milk with 1 teaspoon of vinegar stirred into it. Add the sifted ingredients to the cake mixture in small quantities alternately with milk.

If you wish, stir in ¾ cup of seedless raisins. When these are stirred in, add and thoroughly mix in the beaten whites of the eggs. Bake in cup cake tins in a moderate oven and when hot from the oven spread with the following:

Mix ¼ cup of cocoa with 1¾ cups of confectioner's sugar and stir in just enough hot black coffee (or use hot water if you wish) to make a paste that can be spread over the top of the hot cup cakes. EG

White Nut Cake

- ¾ cup shortening
- 1½ cups sugar
- 2¾ cups sifted flour
- 3 teaspoons baking powder
- ½ teaspoon salt
- 1 cup milk
- ½ teaspoon cream of tartar
- 1 teaspoon vanilla flavoring
- 1 cup nuts, chopped
- 4 eggs whites, stiffly beaten

Cream shortening with sugar. Sift flour with baking powder, salt, and cream of tartar. Add alternately with milk to first mixture. Beat thoroughly. Add flavoring and nuts. Carefully fold in egg whites. Pour into well oiled layer cake pans. Bake in moderate oven 375° for 30 minutes.   EG

Layer Cake

- 4 eggs beaten until light
- 2 cups sugar ⎫
- ½ cup butter ⎬ —cream together
- 1 cup milk
- 3 cups flour ⎫
- 3 teaspoons baking powder ⎬ —sift together

Bake in oven 375°.   MRS. HST

Cream Cake

- 1 pound flour
- 1 pound sugar
- ½ pound butter
- ½ pint cream
- 7 eggs

Beat the yolks and whites well together, add them to the butter, sugar after they are beaten and stir in the other ingredients. Add spice.

NB—I forget whether there is brandy.   IPC

Tea Cake (to be eaten while warm)

- 1 cup flour
- ½ cup sugar
- ½ cup heavy sour cream
- ½ cup raisins
- 1 egg well beaten
- ½ teaspoon baking powder
- ½ teaspoon soda

Mix flour and sugar, add sour cream into which soda has been stirred, then add egg, then baking powder and lastly raisins. Spread in shallow pan, sprinkle thickly with brown sugar and cinnamon. Bake in moderate oven. MCE

Apple Sauce Cake

- 1¾ cups flour
- 1 teaspoon soda
- ¼ teaspoon salt
- 1 teaspoon cinnamon
- ½ teaspoon cloves
- ½ cup butter (or part Crisco)
- 1 cup sugar
- 1 egg well beaten
- 1 cup currants
- 1 cup raisins
- 1 cup hot thick apple sauce

Sift flour once, add soda, salt, spices, and sift 3 times, cream shortening, add egg, raisins, currants, then flour alternately with apple sauce. Bake in greased loaf pan in moderate oven 350° for one hour. No frosting, but top may be decorated with candied cherries, and halves of pecan nuts before baking. EG

Loaf Cake

Take 4½ pounds flour, wet it with ½ pint of yeast water, rose water, wine and brandy. When this mixture is quite light take 2 pounds butter, 2 pounds sugar, 20 eggs beaten as for pound cake, then mix the batter with the sugar, butter and eggs, add 2 pounds currants, mace, cloves and cinnamon to the taste. Bake it as pound cake. IPC

Soft Gingerbread or Spiced Cake

½ cup butter
½ cup boiling water
1 cup dark molasses
¼ teaspoonful salt
1 good teaspoonful cinnamon
¼ teaspoonful of allspice
¼ teaspoonful of cloves
1 heaping teaspoonful of ginger

(plain spice cake without ginger)

1 teaspoonful of soda
1½ scant cups of flour

Melt the butter in the boiling water. Then stir in the molasses, next add salt and spices. Dissolve the soda in a little boiling water and stir thoroughly into mixture. Then stir in the flour, beating all together. Place in buttered pan and bake a half hour in moderate oven. MC

Queen Cake or Pound Cake

1½ pounds butter beat to a cream
2 pounds sugar rolled fine
20 eggs, yolks and whites beaten separately
2 pounds flour sifted
2 wineglasses of brandy, 2 of wine
a nutmeg and some currants CPR

Lady Cake

1 cup of butter, one of cream, 2 of sugar, 3 of flour. 1 small teaspoonful of soda, dissolved in a little warm water, 2 teaspoons cream of tartar, which must be mixed dry in the flour. 1 ounce of bitter almonds mixed with a tablespoon of rose water. Mix all of the ingredients thoroughly, just before baking, add the whites of eight eggs well beaten and the almonds must be grated. IPC

Loaf Spice Cake

- ½ cup shortening
- 1 cup granulated sugar
- 2 eggs
- 1¾ cup sifted cake flour
- ½ teaspoon salt
- 2 teaspoons baking powder
- 2 teaspoons cinnamon
- 1 teaspoon allspice
- 1 teaspoon nutmeg
- ½ teaspoon powdered cloves
- ½ cup plus 2 tablespoons milk

Cream shortening and gradually add sugar. Add eggs unbeaten, one at a time. Add the mixed and sifted dry ingredients alternately with the milk. Bake in a greased loaf pan in a moderate oven of 350° for one hour. ABH

Eggless Cup Cakes

- 2 cups brown sugar ⎫
- ½ cup butter ⎬ cream together
- ½ cup cocoa
- ½ cup boiling water
- 1 teaspoon soda ⎫
- 1 cup sour milk ⎬ mix together
- 2¼ cups flour
- 2 teaspoons vanilla

Bake in 375° in paper cake cups—about 20 minutes.

MRS. HST

Orange Cake

- 2 cups sugar
- 4 eggs (beat separately)
- 2 cups flour
- ½ cup cold water
- pinch of salt
- 2 teaspoons baking powder
- juice and rind of an orange

Bake in layers and ice with orange icing. MRS. L

Sunshine Cake

4	eggs	1	teaspoon cream of tartar
1½	cups flour	1	tablespoon cold water
1½	cups sugar	½	cup boiling water

Beat egg whites

Beat egg yolks, sugar and cold water for 10 minutes. Add dry ingredients after sifting twice. Fold in egg whites and boiling water. Bake for 1 hour in a moderate oven.

Rinse tin with cold water before pouring in mixture.   CPR

Puff Cake

3	eggs	1½	teaspoons baking powder
⅔	cup butter	1¼	cups sugar
2	cups cake flour		vanilla, a pinch of mace
1	cup milk		

Bake in two pans about 20 minutes.

ICING

2	egg whites	½	teaspoon cream of tartar
1½	cups sugar	1	teaspoon vanilla
5	tablespoons cold water		

Put sugar and water on stove, add cream of tartar, then egg whites, beaten stiff. Beat with rotary beater until thoroughly mixed. Cook seven minutes beating constantly or until frosting will stand in peaks. Remove from fire and add flavoring and beat until thick enough to spread.   JJ

Queen Cakes

6	ounces flour	1	teaspoon baking powder
4	ounces butter	2	eggs
3	ounces castor sugar		

Beat butter, sugar to a cream, add eggs one by one and beat well. Add flour by degrees. Sultana or glacé cherries may be added.   CPR

Refrigerator Cheese Cake

- ¼ cup melted butter
- ¼ cup sugar
- 2 cups graham cracker crumbs
- 2 tablespoons gelatin
- 3 eggs separated
- 2 cups dry cottage cheese
- 3 tablespoons lemon juice
- ½ cup sugar
- ¼ teaspoon salt
- 1 tablespoon grated lemon rind
- ½ cup top milk or cream

Blend the butter, one fourth cup sugar and cracker crumbs. Press ¾ of this mixture on bottom and sides of a spring form pan, or large pie pan. Soak gelatin in one half cup of cold water for five minutes. Cook egg yolks, one half cup sugar and remaining water over low heat, stirring constantly until mixture coats a metal spoon. Add gelatin and stir until dissolved. Press dry cheese through a sieve and add custard mixture to cheese. Add lemon juice, rind and salt, beat thoroughly. Cool. When beginning to congeal, beat several minutes with an egg beater. Add cream and fold in stiffly beaten egg whites. Blend thoroughly. Pour into crumb-lined pan. Sprinkle remaining crumbs over the top. Chill until firm.

Brown Sugar Cake

- 2 cups brown sugar
- 1 tablespoon shortening (lard or butter)
- 1 cup sour milk
- ½ teaspoon baking powder
- ½ teaspoon soda
- 2¾ cups flour (sifted)
- 1 teaspoon flavoring

Mix brown sugar, shortening, egg yolks, after beating add milk and flavoring. Then mix flour, sprinkle of salt and baking powder and beat two minutes. MRS. L

Nut Cake

    2 cups sugar (light brown or granulated)
    3 eggs   3 cups flour
    ½ cup shortening   3 teaspoons baking powder
    1 pinch salt   1 cup nuts
    1 cup milk

Cream shortening and sugar. Add eggs, one at a time. Sift and combine dry ingredients and add alternately with milk. Add nuts. Bake in oven 350° for ¾ hour.   ABH

Snow-Flake Cake or Angel Food

    2 cups powdered sugar   10 eggs, whites only
    1 heaping cup prepared flour   flavor to taste.

Beat the eggs stiff, mix in the sugar, flavoring and a little salt, finally the flour. Beat lightly and quickly, and bake at once in two loaves, or in layers for jelly cake.

If ordinary flour is used, add a little baking powder (about ½ teaspoonful). This is a good cake for ice cream, as it is very delicate.   CPR

Sponge Cake

Take 12 eggs—beat the whites and yolks separately. Weigh the eggs before they are broken and add equal quantity of sugar (1 pound) and half as much flour. Put in a little rose-water and orange peel. Bake them in Queen cake pans—before they are put in the oven, sift sugar over them.

Scotch Cakes

    ¼ lb. butter
    ½ lb. flour (slightly less)
    2 oz. sugar

Mix together—roll thin and cut and bake in moderate oven.

Baking Powder Coffee Cake

1 cup sugar	½ cup milk
¼ cup soft butter	1½ cups flour
2 eggs	1 teaspoon baking powder

Cream butter and sugar. Add yolks well beaten and flour sifted with baking powder, alternately with milk. Fold in beaten whites. Pour into greased oblong tin, spread with melted butter, sprinkle with sugar, cinnamon and grated almonds. Bake in moderate oven.   CPR

Strawberry Shortcake

1 quart flour	3 teaspoons baking powder
½ cup pulverized sugar	1 large pinch salt

Mix together, rub in ½ cup butter. Moisten with one egg well beaten and mixed with milk. Do not make dough too soft. Pat out thin and bake in moderately hot oven. Slice the cakes in half and fill the layers with crushed sweetened strawberries and cover with same and top with sweetened whipped cream.   CPR

Graham Cracker Cookies

Butter heavily thin graham crackers. Then sprinkle plentifully with brown sugar. Place under broiler, quite close to fire, for about two or three minutes or until sugar is melted.   MC

Brown Sugar Cookies

- 4 cups brown sugar
- 1 cup shortening
- 4 eggs
- 1 teaspoon cream of tartar & 1 teaspoon salt in 7 cups flour
- 1 teaspoon soda in ¼ cup hot water
- 1 teaspoon vanilla

Mix in evening and form into 2 or 3 long rolls. In the morning slice off and bake.   MRS. MB

Molasses Cookies

    1 cup molasses
    ½ cup lard
    ½ cup sweet milk
    1 teaspoon soda and a little ginger
    flour to make a soft dough

Roll out to about ¼ inch thick and cut with cookie cutter. Beat an egg in a cup and spread on top of cookies with a teaspoon.
                    AUNT FANNIE H

Fancy Sugar Cookies

    1 cup butter   1 tablespoon water
    1 cup sugar   1 teaspoon vanilla
    2 eggs   1 level teaspoon baking powder
    enough flour to make a dough to roll thin

Cream butter and sugar thoroughly with wooden spoon. Beat eggs until very light and add to creamed mixture, beat well and add water and extract. To ½ cup sifted flour add baking powder and sift into other ingredients. Beat until light then add enough flour to make soft dough, about 2 level cupfuls. Turn onto baking board, knead lightly and roll thin. Bake in quick oven—will keep indefinitely.
                    MRS. TEB

Ginger Cookies

    1 cup butter   ½ teaspoon allspice
    1 cup sugar   ½ teaspoon cinnamon
    1 cup molasses   ½ teaspoon cloves
    2 cups flour   ¼ teaspoon baking soda
    2 teaspoons ginger   ¼ teaspoon salt

Put sugar, butter and molasses in a pan to soften. Add the spices. Put away until hard enough. Use more flour to roll out—a little at a time, very thin.

Bake in a slow oven for 15 or 20 minutes.
                    CPR

Peanut Butter Cookies

½ cup granulated sugar	1 egg
½ cup brown sugar	1 cup flour
½ cup butter or shortening	½ teaspoon soda
½ cup nuts or cocoanut	½ teaspoon vanilla
½ cup peanut butter	pinch of salt

Roll a teaspoon of dough into a ball and place on cookie sheet. Flatten with prongs of fork and bake 15 minutes in moderate oven. Makes about 35 cookies.   MRS. MB

Oatmeal Cookies

1 cup butter (or margarine)
2 cups granulated sugar
2 beaten eggs
1 teaspoonful vanilla
1 teaspoonful salt
¼ teaspoonful soda
3 cups quick cooking oatmeal
½ cup chopped walnuts

Thoroughly cream butter and sugar; add eggs and vanilla—beat well. Add sifted dry ingredients, and then oatmeal. Mix well. Put 1 teaspoonful of mixture for each cookie spaced far apart on greased cookie sheet. Bake 20 to 30 minutes at 350°.
   MC

Chocolate Cookies (Aunt Ruth's)

3 cups brown sugar ⎫
¾ cup butter and lard ⎬ —cream
3 eggs beaten
4 squares chocolate melted

1 teaspoon soda. Mix in 3 teaspoons of thick milk. Add flour to make a stiff dough, then roll out thin and cut with a cookie cutter. After they are baked, spread with a stiff white icing and sprinkle with chocolate decorettes, shredded cocoanut or colored sugar. These are the children's favorite Christmas cookie.   MRS. MB

Swedish Orange Cookies

Cream ½ cup butter
Add scant cup sugar
Grated rind of 1 orange and 1 tablespoon orange juice
Add 3 egg yolks and enough flour to make it stiff enough to knead. Chill over night—cut thin—brush with beaten egg or egg white and decorate with cherries, nuts or what you have. Bake 375°. Will keep indefinitely in tight tin.   MRS. TEB

Josephine's Oatmeal Cookies

One big cupful of butter, one big cupful of sugar, two eggs, one cupful of raisins, three-fourths tablespoon of cinnamon, two cupfuls of oatmeal (Mother's Oats), five tablespoons of milk, one-fourth teaspoonful of baking soda, one cupful of flour. Stir all together. Put little dabs of the mixture from a tablespoon in a pan. Cook in oven about fifteen minutes.   LBM

Pecan Cookies

½ cup butter	1 beaten egg
1 cup brown sugar	½ teaspoon vanilla
1 cup flour	½ cup broken nuts

Drop from spoon on buttered cookie tin.   MRS. HST

Spekulatins, A good crisp spice cookie

- 2 cups sugar
- 1 large cup butter
- 2 eggs
- 2 tablespoons sour cream mixed with
- 2 teaspoons baking soda
- 1 teaspoon baking powder mixed with
- 5 cups flour
- 1½ teaspoons cinnamon

Roll out thin and cut with a cookie cutter and bake in a moderate oven.   MRS. AH

Fudge Cookies

- 2 squares chocolate
- 1 cup sugar or 1½ cup brown sugar
- 2 eggs—beaten
- 4 tablespoons milk
- 1 cup flour
- ¼ cup butter
- 1 teaspoon vanilla
- 1 cup chopped nuts

Cream butter and sugar. Add eggs and milk and flour alternately. Add melted chocolate, nuts and flavoring. Spread about one-quarter inch thick in pan. Moderate oven—cut in squares.

VP

Cookies

- 1 can Eagle condensed milk
- 6 cups Post Toasties
- 1 package chocolate drops

Put milk in bowl—add chocolates and stir—then add Post Toasties, trying not to mash them. Drop on greased cookie pan and cook about 15 or 20 minutes in 350°.

Christmas Crisps

- ⅔ pound brown sugar
- ½ pound butter
- 2 eggs, unbeaten
- 2 cups sifted cake flour
- ⅓ teaspoon soda
- ½ pound pecans, ground fine

Cream butter and sugar until light, add eggs, then flour, then soda dissolved in small amount of water. Put ½ pecan in centre of each teaspoon of batter dropped on the greased tin, and bake in moderate oven for about 10 minutes.

MCE

Ginger Snaps

1 cup molasses, 1 teaspoon of baking soda, ½ cup of sugar, ½ cup of butter, 1 teaspoon of ginger, 3 cups flour. Mix molasses, sugar, ginger, butter over fire and stir until butter is melted, then pour into pan quickly and cool. Add other ingredients and form into long roll. Slice off thin slices and bake 8 or 10 minutes in quick oven.

CM

Nut Wafers

    1 cup brown sugar   1 cup nuts
    1 tablespoon butter   about 8 tablespoons flour
    2 eggs   1 teaspoon baking powder

Roll thin and bake in moderate oven about 12 minutes.

AUNT FANNIE H

Soft Gingerbread

- 1 cup butter and lard
- 2 eggs
- 1 cup brown sugar
- 1 cup sour milk, cream or buttermilk
- 1 cup New Orleans molasses
- 1 tablespoon ginger
- 1 teaspoon cinnamon
- ½ teaspoon cloves
- 2 teaspoons soda dissolved in a little hot water
- Grated rind of 1 lemon
- 3½ cups flour

Stir butter, sugar, and eggs together, add other ingredients, leaving soda until last. In absence of sour milk, use the sweet and add the juice of the lemon.

MRS. E

Ginger Bread

    ½ cup granulated sugar   1 tablespoon ginger
    1 cup baking molasses   ½ cup butter
    ½ teaspoon cloves   2½ cups flour
    2 teaspoons soda dissolved in 1 cup boiling water
    2 eggs

Cream butter and sugar. Add molasses and mix. Sift ginger, cloves with flour and mix. Then add water and soda. Last well-beaten eggs. After in pan, sprinkle with 1 cup chopped or whole nuts. Moderate oven about 40 minutes. Line pan with heavy waxed paper. This batter is very thin but very good. Use a pan about 8 x 12 inches.

VP

Soft Gingerbread

- ½ cup butter and lard mixed
- 1 cup brown sugar
- 1 egg
- 1 cup dark cooking molasses
- 1 cup sour cream or buttermilk
- 2 teaspoons baking soda dissolved in boiling water
- 2½ cups flour
- Cinnamon and cloves to taste—plenty of each
- Raisins and currants may be added

Mix ingredients in order given. Bake at about 375° for ¾ hour, then test with broom straw to see if done. This is too soft to turn out of pans. Does well in 2 9-inch layer cake pans.

MDB

Tarts

- ½ pound butter
- ¼ cup milk
- 2 cream cheeses

Enough flour to hold together—roll thin—cut with biscuit cutter and prick with fork. Bake in hot oven.

Slice fruit, put in thick syrup and boil for 10 or 15 minutes. Take slices out with strainer—place slices on the crusts. Boil down syrup remaining until almost stiff and brush over fruit and put in oven for a few minutes.

CPR

German Sand Tarts

- 2 cups butter
- 2½ cups sugar
- 4 cups flour
- 2 eggs well beaten
- 1 egg white

Cream butter and sugar together, slowly add flour, working in well—add beaten eggs and mix thoroughly. Chill over night. Roll thin, brush with slightly beaten egg white. Sprinkle with sugar and cinnamon and decorate with nuts. Bake in moderate oven 350° for 10 minutes.

MRS. TEB

Cherry Macaroons

1 cup ground, blanched almonds
1 cup sugar
3 unbeaten egg whites
¼ pound candied cherries, cut very fine.

Rub the almonds to a paste with the sugar, add egg whites and then the cherries. Mix well and drop from teaspoon on a greased cookie sheet. Garnish each cookie with a piece of candied cherry and bake in a moderate oven for 20 minutes. Store in tin container. Makes about 3 dozen. **EG**

Macaroons

1 pound almond paste
6 whites of eggs (unbeaten)
1 pound of sugar (½ powdered and ½ granulated)

Cut almond paste into thin slices and gradually work in the whites of 3 eggs, then mix in the sugar thoroughly. Add the remaining egg whites, part at a time until mixture is free from lumps. With 2 spoons make small thick drops about size of quarter, 2 inches apart on clean dry brown paper (never wax paper) placed in shallow pan. Bake in a moderately hot oven—325°—until light brown. Don't bake too much or they will become brittle. After baking dampen underside of paper, let stand before removing.

Cheese Cake Pie

2 cups cottage cheese
½ cup milk
3 eggs
½ cup sugar
little nutmeg
1 teaspoon melted butter

Press cheese through a colander, beat eggs until light, add them with all other ingredients to the cheese; beat until smooth, line a deep pie dish with plain paste, fill with this mixture, bake about thirty minutes. Sprinkle a little cinnamon on top.

Date and Nut Bread

- 2¼ cups sifted flour
- 1½ teaspoons baking powder
- ¾ teaspoon soda
- ½ teaspoon salt
- ¼ cup sugar
- 1 cup chopped nuts
- 1 cup chopped pitted dates
- 1 cup boiling water
- ½ cup light corn syrup
- 2 tablespoons melted lard
- 1 egg

Oil a five by nine inch loaf pan. Sift together the flour, soda, salt, baking powder and sugar. Add nuts. Pour boiling water over dates, add syrup, melted lard and beaten egg. Add liquid to dry ingredients, stirring as little as possible. Pour into the pans. Bake in a slow oven, 325°, for one hour and 15 minutes.

EG

Angel Food Waldorf

Combine 1½ pints of whipping cream, 6 tablespoons sugar, 6 tablespoons cocoa and salt and chill for an hour. Then whip mixture stiff.

- 1 cup blanched almonds

Place cake with larger surface at bottom on a large serving plate. Cut entire top from cake about ¾ inch from top. Remove center from main part of cake by cutting down into the cake about ¾ inch from side and ¾ inch from middle hole, leaving a ¾ wall. Remove this center with curved knife or spoon being careful to leave a wall of cake at bottom. Fill cavity with ⅓ of chocolate cream mixture, to which has been added half of the nuts, cut coarsely. Replace top, spread remaining cream on top and sides. Shave rest of nuts and sprinkle over top and sides of cake. Chill for three hours before serving.

New York Tea Biscuit

3 pounds of flour	1 tablespoon of carraway seeds
1½ pounds of sugar	1 teaspoon potash
1 pound butter	½ pint of milk

Irish Tea Biscuits

2 cups all purpose flour
½ teaspoon salt
1 tablespoon baking powder
¼ cup shortening (lard or vegetable)
⅔ to ¾ cup milk
1 cup currants

Add solid shortening to the sifted dry ingredients, mix with blender, until mixture resembles coarse meal; add currants, then stir in milk until dough follows fork around bowl. Turn out on floured board, knead gently so it will not be sticky to handle. Roll out lightly, cut with biscuit cutter, bake on ungreased baking sheet in hot oven 450° 12 to 15 minutes. Makes 14 biscuits.

EG

Sherry Meringues

To each egg white beaten stiff add 1 cup sugar, 1 teaspoon cornstarch, 2 tablespoons sherry, walnut meats or cocoanut.

Drop on soda crackers and bake in 400° until light brown. Serve with fruit, or ice cream.

Jackson Jumbles

3 cups sugar	1 cup butter
5 cups flour	1 cup cream
1 teaspoon baking powder	2 eggs

Sift flour, sugar and baking powder together, into them rub the butter, then add cream and well-beaten eggs, roll as thin as possible and bake in moderate oven.

MCE

Sponge Cake

10 to 12 eggs
1 pound granulated sugar
juice of 1½ lemons
½ pound flour

Separate whites and beat them very, very light in a large bowl. Add yolks one at a time, stir in the sugar and then keep beating well. Add lemon juice and beat some more. Stir in the flour rapidly but very quietly, after sifting it well. Do not beat after adding flour. Bake in slow oven 1½ hours.

MO

Chocolate Velvet Frosting

3 squares Baker's unsweetened chocolate
1½ cups sifted confectioner's sugar
2½ tablespoons hot water
3 egg yolks
4 tablespoons butter or margarine

Melt chocolate in double boiler. Remove from heat, add sugar and water. Add egg yolks and beat thoroughly. Then add butter and continue beating until smooth. Makes enough frosting to cover tops and sides of two 8 or 9 inch layers, or top and sides of 10 x 10 x 2 inch cake, or tube pan. ABH

MEMORANDA

MEMORANDA

MEMORANDA

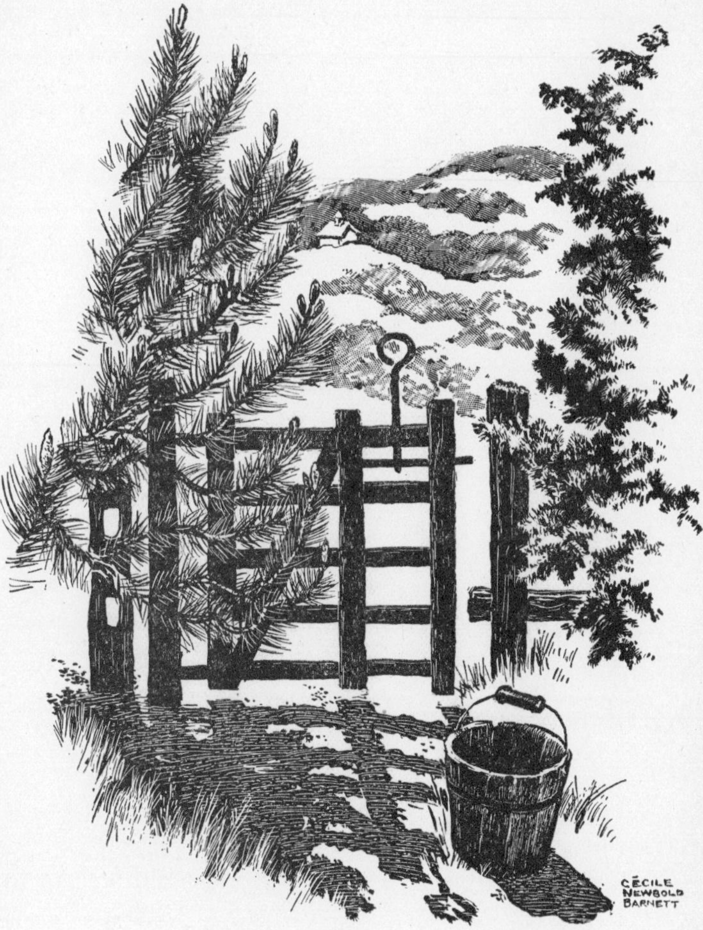
CÉCILE
NEWBOLD
BARNETT

DESSERTS

Dumplings Fried in Caramel Syrup

Syrup:
- 1 cup brown sugar ⎫
- ½ cup hot water ⎬ —boil 2 minutes and pour into baking dish
- 2 tablespoons butter ⎭

Dumplings:
- ¼ cup sugar
- 2 tablespoons butter
- 1 egg
- ½ teaspoon vanilla
- 1¾ cups flour
- 2 teaspoons baking powder

Cream butter and sugar. Add egg, milk and vanilla. Add sifted flour and stir until mixed. Drop by spoonful into pan of syrup and bake in hot oven for 2 minutes and serve hot with whipped cream.

Chocolate Roll

- 3 eggs
- ½ cup sugar
- 2 tablespoons flour
- 2 tablespoons cocoa
- ½ pint heavy cream

Beat eggs separately. Sift dry ingredients together (flour and cocoa). Beat yolks with most of sugar, save a little to beat with whites, add pinch of salt. Bake on cookie sheet. Turn cake on sugared wax paper, spread on whipped cream and roll. Chill in refrigerator and slice.

EAC

Boston Cream Pie

- 1½ cups flour
- 2 level teaspoons baking powder
- ¼ teaspoon salt
- 2 tablespoons of sugar
- ¾ cup of milk
- 1 egg
- 2 tablespoons melted shortening

Sift the dry ingredients into bowl and add milk, beaten egg and melted shortening, mix well. Brush two layer cake tins with shortening and dust with flour, pour in mixture and smooth top. Put in hot oven, bake 15 to 20 minutes.

FILLING

- 2 cups milk
- 2 tablespoons of cornstarch
- 3 tablespoons sugar
- 1 teaspoon vanilla or flavoring of your own taste.
- 1 egg
- pinch of salt

Put milk on to boil, mix cornstarch, sugar and salt, with a little milk, then add the well beaten egg. Add to the boiling milk, boil 3 minutes, when partly cooled, spread between layers, dust top with powdered sugar. CM

Almond Pudding

- 6 eggs
- 1 cup sugar
- ¾ cup flour
- about ½ or ¾ cup chopped almonds
- 1 quart milk
- pinch of salt

Mix egg yolks and sugar. Beat well. Add flour.

Scald milk and add salt and almonds. To scalded milk add the first mixture. Boil until an even thickness. Remove from fire and add vanilla and well-beaten egg whites. Cool in individual sauce dishes or large dish as desired. Serve with warm cherry sauce or fresh strawberries mashed and sweetened.

Bread Pudding

4 eggs beaten, one quart of milk, sugar and vanilla to taste. 4 pieces of stale bread or crusts buttered, put in pudding pan, then in another pan with a little water to create a steam, cook in oven at medium heat about 30 minutes, try with knife to see if it custards, if cooked too long it will curdle. CM

Dessert Wine Jelly

On a half box of gelatin put half pint of cold water. Let it stand an hour. Add 1 pound of sugar and half pint of sherry wine, juice of two lemons and a little rind. Pour 1½ pints of boiling water on this and stir well and strain through muslin and cool. (Knox gelatine does not need to soak and ¾ of one package. The great thing is not to have too much water.)
ST

Danish Lemon Pudding

    2 tablespoons gelatin   1 cup sugar
    3 tablespoons cold water   grated rind of one lemon
    ½ cup boiling water   juice from 1½ lemons
    5 eggs—separated   ½ pint cream whipped

Soften gelatin in cold water. Add boiling water. Stir until dissolved. Beat egg yolks. Add sugar. Beat until creamy. Mix grated lemon rind and juice. Stir into mixture. Add the cool gelatin. Pour into mold. Chill until firm. Serve with whipped cream.

Lemon Sponge Pie

    1 cup sugar   1 cup milk
    2 tablespoons butter   1 lemon—rind and juice
    2 tablespoons flour   2 eggs

Cream sugar, butter, egg yolks together, add flour, lemon juice, and rind; then stir milk in slowly. Beat the 2 egg whites stiff, fold gently into mixture, pour into unbaked pie shell. Bake in moderate oven 375° for 45 minutes. EG

A Cream Pudding

Put into a saucepan a quart of very rich cream, grate into it some nutmeg, break in two blades of mace, add four cloves whole, and a good piece of sharp cinnamon; then add a very little salt and one spoonful of powdered sugar; set it on the fire, and let it once boil up then put in the crust of two French rolls cut into very thin slices; let it stand till cold. Then pour off what cream is not soaked into the bread; put this bread into a strainer, and press the fine part through the holes into a China dish; break six eggs, separate two of the whites, but let all the rest go in; mix this with the cream pap; butter a dish and put it in, tie a cloth over it, and put it into a pot of clean water; let it boil five and thirty minutes, then take it out and serve with butter.

A Fine Plain Pudding

Gather six fresh Laurel leaves that are not too old and hard, nor so near the tops of the branches as to be quite soft and tender; they should for this use be of a pale green, and tolerable firm; boil these in a quart of milk; when it has once boiled up take out the leaves, put in as much flour as will make it into a kind of thick hasty-pudding; then take it off the fire, and stir in half a pound of fine fresh butter, add a quarter of a pound of loaf sugar powdered, and grate in a little nutmeg. Break twelve eggs, put six of them into a basin yolks and whites together, and put in the yolks only of the other six; beat all these well together, and butter a dish ready, pour in the whole, and bake half an hour and it will come out as fine a pudding of its kind as art can produce.

Raisin Pie

1 egg
1 cup raisins
5 or 6 common crackers
½ cup milk
1 teaspoon salt
⅓ cup sugar
1 tablespoon cocoanut
small lump butter on top
2 crusts

EH

A Fine Rice Pudding—Superb!

Clean some rice, blanch it in water, and then set it on in milk proportioned to the quantity of the rice; put in some salt at first, and when it is half boiled break in a large stick of cinnamon, let it boil some time longer with this, and then add some fine sugar powdered.

When the rice is boiled tender, and the whole is thick, take it from the fire. Pick and wash half a pound of currants, and stone the same quantity of the finest raisins of the sun. Beat up six eggs with three of the whites, mix these with the rice and milk, and then put in the currants and raisins, and stir all well together. Break a pair of good beef marrow bones, take out the marrow cut it into small square pieces, and stir these in; then put it into a dish and bake. This is a very delicate pudding, and is fit to appear at any table. Suet may be used instead of marrow, but it is much inferior to it. And for a dish intended to be elegant the difference in the effort is not much minded.

¾ cup rice—1 quart milk—½ cup sugar—½ cup currants—½ cup raisins—5 egg yolks

A Rice Pudding for Baking

Pick a pound of rice very clean, and boil it in water till it is just tender; then pour it into a cloth, put over the top of a pan, and let all the water run gently from it without squeezing. While it is hot, and when it is pretty well drained, stir in a good piece of butter; then add some fine sugar, and a little salt; grate in some nutmeg, and season it in all these respects to the palate, tasting at times, and adding where the quantity is not sufficient of any kind. Wash and pick half a pound of currants, and when all the rest is well mixed, put these in; stir all very well together, and then prepare a pan to hold it. Butter the inside of it very well, pour in the ingredients, and set it into the oven, let it be well baked; it will come out of a fine brown, mellow and very pleasant.

A Boiled Loaf

Put a loaf of bread into a pan and pour upon it a pint of milk boiling hot. Let it stand till all the milk is soaked up, and then tie it up in a bag and boil it a quarter of an hour; this will do it sufficiently. Take it out of the bag, lay it in a warm dish, and pour over it some melted butter; throw some fine sugar over this, and then squeeze over it a Seville orange. If a little white wine be mixed in the butter while it is melting it will improve it, and if the orange juice be done in the same manner it eats well.

Company Dessert

Cream together ½ cup shortening, ½ cup sugar; add 4 egg yolks beaten and 1 teaspoon vanilla. Sift together 1 cup flour, 1 teaspoon baking powder, ¼ teaspoon salt and add alternately with 5 tablespoons milk. Spread in 2 eight inch layer cake pans, greased and floured. Beat 4 egg whites stiff, add 1 cup sugar gradually. Beat thoroughly. Spread over each layer, cover with chopped walnuts. Bake ½ hour in moderate oven 325°. Turn out carefully. Cool, then put layers together with custard filling. Combine 2 tablespoons sugar, 1 tablespoon cornstarch, pinch salt, 1 egg yolk, 1 cup milk, cook until thick. Add ½ teaspoon vanilla. EG

Honey Boy

¼ cup shredded cocoanut	½ square chocolate
¾ cup raisins	2 cups flaked bran
½ package pitted dates	¾ tablespoons honey

Put cocoanut, raisins, dates, alternately through food chopper. Stir in melted chocolate, then bran and honey alternately. Form mixture into a roll about one-inch in diameter; put in cold place. Cut in slices with sharp knife. The roll keeps fresh for several days if wrapped in wax paper and stored in a tightly covered container. Small balls of above mixture may be dipped in melted fondant. EG

Trifle

    2 cups stale cake, cut in small cubes
    ¼ cup currant or grape jelly

CUSTARD SAUCE

Place one-third of the cake cubes in the bottom of a bowl; dot over with 2 tablespoons of the jelly. Add one-half the remaining cake cubes and dot over with the remaining jelly. Top with remaining cake cubes and pour chilled custard over all. Chill and serve in individual dishes, each topped with a bit of jelly. Makes 4 servings.

Note: If preferred, strips of sponge cake may be spread with the jelly and arranged in sherbert glasses. Then pour in the custard sauce. Chill   EG

Cinnamon Fluff

    2 tablespoons butter   1 scant cup milk
    1 cup sugar   2 teaspoons baking powder
    2 eggs   about 2 cups flour

Pour into pans 7 x 12 and dot with butter. Sprinkle over all a generous amount of cinnamon and sugar. Bake in quick oven. This is very good eaten hot with tea. Does not keep well. The batter is quite thin.   MHC

Hot Milk Sponge Cake

    4 eggs   1 lump butter melted in milk
    2 teaspoons baking powder   2 cups sugar
    1 cup scalding milk   2 cups flour

Beat egg whites stiff—add yolks, beat well—add sugar slowly. Beat until almost dissolved—add flour, baking powder, salt which have been sifted together—add hot milk and butter. Flavor as desired (vanilla or almond). Do not beat batter after flour is added. This makes a thin batter. Bake 350° oven for 50 minutes in tube pan or three layer cake tins.

    EMT

Rhubarb Crunch

Mix until crumbly
- 1 cup sifted flour
- ¾ cup oatmeal (uncooked)
- 1 cup brown sugar—firmly packed
- ½ cup melted butter
- 1 teaspoon cinnamon

Press half of crumbs into greased 9-inch pan. Cover with 4 cups diced rhubarb.

Combine
- 1 cup sugar
- 2 tablespoons cornstarch
- 1 cup water
- 1 teaspoon vanilla

Cook until thick and clear
Pour over rhubarb
Top with remaining crumbs.
Bake 350° for one hour.
Cut in squares and serve with whipped cream.   FR

Ice Cream Snow Balls

- 1 quart vanilla ice cream
- ⅔ cup finely chopped pecans or walnuts

Make large snowballs of vanilla ice cream using scoop or large spoon, roll each one quickly in chopped nuts. Serve plain or with butterscotch sauce as follows:

- 1 cup brown sugar
- ¼ cup milk
- 2 tablespoons corn syrup
- 3 tablespoons butter
- pinch of salt

Combine above ingredients in sauce pan, heat to boiling to about 200° about 3 minutes. Serve over ice cream balls.   EG

Roll ice cream balls in chocolate cake crumbs, or other stale cake. Serve with chocolate sauce.   VP

Apple Batter Pudding

 4 to 5 tart apples   1 egg
 ¼ cup sugar   ½ cup sugar
 2 tablespoons butter   1 tablespoon softened butter
 ½ teaspoon cinnamon   ¼ cup bread flour
 ¼ cup hot water   1 teaspoon baking powder
 2 tablespoons butter

Core and pare apples and cut in slices, crosswise. Put into a deep pudding dish, sprinkle with sugar and cinnamon, add two tablespoons butter cut in small pieces and pour water over the top. Spread over the top a batter made as follows:

Beat the egg light, add the sugar gradually and continue beating, then the softened butter and last the flour mixed with baking powder. Dot over the top of the batter with two more tablespoons butter, and bake in a moderately hot oven (400°) until the apples are soft; this will take about a half hour. Serve with cream from a pitcher or with a hard sauce. Serves 6.   EG

Date Cookies

 1 cup brown sugar (pressed in)
 ⅔ cup butter
 ¼ teaspoon salt
 2 eggs
 1 tablespoon vinegar
 2 cups sifted flour
 ½ teaspoon soda
 ½ teaspoon baking powder
 1 pound dates (cut each in 3 pieces)
 1 cup black walnuts, broken

Cream sugar and butter and salt. Then add eggs. Do not beat them. Mix all together, then add 1 tablespoon of vinegar. Sift the flour, soda and baking powder into the mixture, then mix. Add the dates and nuts and mix. Drop on greased baking sheets with teaspoon. Bake in 350° oven till browned.

               MRS. LFY

Strawberry Pie

Dissolve 1 package of jello in 2 cups water

Hull and sugar 1 quart strawberries. After jello is set stir in the strawberries, put in crust (baked), set in ice box.

Serve with whipped cream. EPM

Apple Torte

  1 tablespoon melted butter
  1 egg
  4 tart cooking apples
  1 cup sugar
  ½ teaspoon vanilla
  ½ cup sifted flour
  2 teaspoons baking powder
  ½ cup nut meats
  ½ cup chopped dates or raisins

Pare and chop apples. Sift dry ingredients together. Combine all ingredients. Spread in a 9 inch square buttered cake pan. Bake in moderate oven (350°) about 30 minutes or until apples are soft. Serve hot or cold with foamy or hard sauce.

EPM

Mrs. Brackbill's Shoo Fly Pie

  1 cup baking molasses
  1 cup boiling water
  1 teaspoon soda

—I use Grandma's molasses. Mix these and let stand while you mix crumbs, cinnamon and nutmeg together.

  3 cups flour
  1 cup sugar
  lard size of an egg

—Mix together till crumbly

Line two large pie plates with dough. Divide the liquid between the two plates. Then sprinkle the crumbs over the top and bake for a half hour or more. MRS. B

Buttermilk Pudding

Heat buttermilk with 2 or 3 handfuls of raisins, stirring constantly till ready to boil. Add sago or minute tapioca to thicken slightly and sweeten to taste. EH

Shoo Fly Pie

- 1 cup molasses
- 1 cup hot water   —mix and let cool
- 1 teaspoon soda
- 1 cup sugar
- ½ cup shortening—not butter   —rub this mixture into crumbs
- 3 cups flour

Use cake pans, line with pastry as for pies, fill with mixture of crumbs and molasses.   Old Chester County recipe.

MRS. SGL

Shoo Fly Pie (Dutch Way)

- 1 cup table molasses
- 1 teaspoon baking soda
- 1 cup warm water

Dissolve soda completely in warm water, beating it into molasses. Pour into pastry lined pie pans.

Have ready mixed:

- 2 cups flour   ¾ teaspoon baking soda
- ½ cup sugar   ¼ to ⅓ cup shortening (not butter)

Mix these ingredients into crumbs, sprinkle evenly over the two pies and bake in pre-heated moderately hot oven 350° about 45 minutes or until done.

EG

Blanc Mange

- jelly from 1 pair calves feet
- 1 pint of cream
- ¼ pound loaf sugar
- 3 blades mace.

Put it over the fire until it boils then strain it in a bowl and when nearly cold add a half glass of wine and rose water. Then pour it in a mould. A few bitter almonds. It should be frequently stirred while cooling to prevent the jelly and cream separating.

Apple Cream Pie

    2 cups tart apples (chopped)   1 egg slightly beaten
    ¾ cup sugar   ½ teaspoon vanilla
    2 teaspoons flour (level)   pinch of salt.
    1 cup thick sour cream

Combine apples, sugar, flour, salt and stir in cream and beaten egg. Mix well. Bake in slow oven until set—350°

Mix ⅓ cup of sugar, ⅔ cup of flour, 1 teaspoon cinnamon, ¼ cup melted butter, make crumbs. Sprinkle on pie after it is baked, set back in oven for 8 minutes to brown. Serve cold.

EG

Sour Cream Peach Pie

    7 or 8 halved peaches   ½ cup granulated sugar
    1 cup thick sour cream   2 tablespoons flour
    1 cup brown sugar   2 tablespoons tapioca

Combine flour, granulated sugar and tapioca. Spread this on bottom and sides of unbaked pie shell. Combine the sour cream and brown sugar and dip each peach section in this mixture and arrange in pie shell. After pie shell is filled, pour the remaining sour cream mixture over the peach sections and place in a preheated oven of 400°. After 15 minutes, reduce temperature and continue baking until peaches are tender.

EG

Black Walnut Nut Bread (3 loaves)

    3 cups granulated sugar
    6 cups sifted flour
    ¼ teaspoon salt
    6 teaspoons baking powder
    3 eggs, well beaten
    3 cups milk
    1 cup cream
    3 cups black walnut, kernels, left large

Mix the solids first, then beat and add the eggs, milk, cream and nut kernels. Bake in moderate oven.   MO

Nesselrode Pie

- 3 eggs, separated
- 1½ cups milk
- 2 teaspoons unflavored gelatine
- 1 tablespoon cold water
- 2 tablespoons rum flavoring
- ¼ cup maraschino cherries, chopped
- 2 tablespoons shaved, sweet chocolate
- ¼ teaspoon salt
- ⅔ cup sugar

One pie shell, baked. Combine slightly beaten egg yolks, milk, salt, ⅓ cup sugar in top of double boiler. Cook over hot, not boiling, water until mixture thickens, stirring constantly; remove from hot water. Soften gelatine in cold water; add to hot mixture; stir until dissolved. Chill until mixture begins to thicken. Beat egg whites stiff but not dry, gradually beat in remaining sugar. Fold into gelatine mixture with rum flavoring and cherries. Pile into baked pastry shell, sprinkle with chocolate, chill until firm.   EG

Baked Indian Pudding (100 years old)

- 2 tablespoons yellow meal
- 1 tablespoon pearl tapioca
- 1 teaspoon ginger
- 1 teaspoon salt
- ½ teaspoon lemon extract
- 1 egg
- ½ cup molasses (black)
- 1 teaspoon butter
- 1 pinch soda
- 1 quart milk

Mix dry ingredients together, stir in half the milk, the molasses and egg well beaten, then rest of milk. Cook in slow oven about two hours. Stir up from bottom 2 or 3 times as it thickens, also stirring in a pint or more of milk or water so it will whey. Brown it on top. Serve with or without whipped cream.   EH

Apple Dowdy (100 years old)

Apples cooked as for sauce. Biscuit dough put on top. After taking off, turn upside down and sprinkle with sugar and cinnamon. Serve with cream and sugar.   EH

Bag Pudding

Take 2 cups wheat flour, 2 cups Indian meal (or corn meal), ½ cup suet chopped fine, 1 cup sugar, 2 heaping teaspoons baking powder and a pinch of salt. Mix flour, corn meal, suet, sugar and salt thoroughly, then add enough milk or water to make the consistency of thick cake batter, and beat well to make fine grained. Last of all add baking powder and merely stir into the batter. Sometimes use 1 quart canned cherries or fruit of any kind instead of the milk or water.

Have a pot of boiling water ready and dip in the pudding bag, wring out, and put in the bag a small handful of flour. Hold the top of bag together with the hand and shake flour over inside of bag thoroughly to keep the pudding from sticking to the bag. Pour the batter into the bag, making only half full, and allowing room for the pudding to swell, and tie top of bag together with a string. Put in pot of boiling water and boil steadily for one hour. When done, lift from pot with a fork, cut string, turn bag inside out and the pudding will drop out easily. Serve with sweetened dip.

This recipe is 100 years old. CEB

Floating Island

Take a pint of currant jelly, the whites of 4 eggs. Beat well together. In hot weather keep the pot in a tub of cool water or in a cool place. Sweeten the milk or cream and when it is stiff enough put it on the top, in a deep china dish.

Aunt Grace's Bread Pudding

2 cups stale bread, cover with cold water and let stand till you heat 1 quart of milk, ¼ cup of butter, ½ teaspoon of salt and ½ cup of sugar. Do not boil, only heat.

Squeeze water out of bread and crumble. Then add to milk. Beat 4 eggs lightly—add 1 teaspoon vanilla and shake of nutmeg. Then add to milk mixture. Bake in greased baking dish 50 to 60 minutes. MRS. B

Cinnamon Flop

- 1 cup 4X sugar
- 1 tablespoon butter
- 1 cup sweet milk
- 1 tablespoon nutmeg ground
- 2 cups flour
- 2 tablespoons baking powder

Bake in two well-greased pans. Dot with butter over top, brown sugar and cinnamon. Let cool in pan. 375°   MRS. HST

Lemon Pie without Meringue

- ½ pound granulated sugar
- ¼ pound butter
- 5 eggs
- 2 lemons, and 2 tablespoons white wine

Beat sugar, butter and yolks. Let this rest for at least a half hour. Then add the whites, well beaten. This makes 3 pies.

MO

Chocolate Cakes 1872

- ¼ pound chocolate, grated
- 1 cup brown sugar
- 1 tablespoon butter
- 1 teaspoon cinnamon
- ¾ teaspoon pulverized cloves
- 1 egg and enough flour to roll out

MO

Crunchy Apple Dessert

- 1 cup sugar
- 1 tablespoon flour
- 1 teaspoon baking powder
- ¼ teaspoon salt

} sift together

- 2 egg yolks
- 1 cup diced apples
- 1 cup chopped nuts
- 1 teaspoon vanilla

Add all ingredients in order given to sifted ones, add 2 egg whites beaten stiff last. Bake 1 hour 335°. Serve hot or cold with whipped cream.

ZP

Christmas Plum Pudding

¾ pound suet chopped very fine
¾ pound seeded raisins
¾ pound currants
¾ pound sugar
¾ pound fresh bread crumbs
Grated zest of one lemon
¼ pound candied citron cut into fine shavings
1 teaspoon each of ground cinnamon, cloves, nutmeg and allspice

Mix the dry materials together thoroughly and flour lightly, then add six eggs mixed well but not beaten and 12 cups of brandy, if too stiff add another egg, if too wet add some more bread crumbs. Wet a strong cloth in cold water, wring it dry and dredge it thoroughly with flour. Turn the mixture into the center and draw the cloth together over the top leaving room for the pudding to swell a little, and tie it firmly; give it a good round shape. Put it into a pot of boiling water, having it completely covered with water, cover the pot and boil four to five hours. Do not let the water fall below the pudding and in adding more water let it be hot so as not to arrest the boiling. After it is removed from the water let it rest in the bag for ten minutes to harden a little, then cut the string and turn it carefully into a dish. Serve with brandy sauce. Pudding can be put aside and kept for some time and then heated up by putting in boiling water. MRS. RC

Chocolate Ice Cream

1 quart milk
2 eggs beaten (not to a froth)
½ teaspoon salt
2 teaspoons vanilla
1 cup granulated sugar

Heat all thoroughly and add 5 large squares of Baker's unsweetened chocolate. When all is melted and blended set aside in kitchen to cool. Not in refrigerator. When quite cold add a quart of heavy cream and freeze in freezer. Let stand several hours in freezer before serving. CPR

Vanilla Ice Cream

   1   quart cream—1 pint top milk
   1½ vanilla beans

Boil beans in ½ pint of the milk for ½ hour. Open and rub them with spoon. Scrape them with knife. 1 cup sugar put in hot milk with vanilla. When cool add rest of milk and cream. Put in freezer and place on ice for an hour, then freeze.   CPR

Strawberry or Peach Ice Cream

Mash and put through coarse strainer and sweeten to taste the fruit desired. Have same quantity of fruit pulp as thin cream. Freeze in freezer.   VP

Floating Island

Take one spoonful of jelly to the whites of two eggs and whip it till light.

Potato Pudding

Boil, peel and mash 2 pounds potatoes, beat them into a smooth batter with ¾ of a pint of milk, 2 ounces moist sugar and 2 or 3 beaten eggs. Bake it ¾ of an hour. 3 ounces of currants or raisins may be added. Leave out the milk and add 3 ounces of butter and it will make a nice cake. Sprinkle with sugar.

Potato Pudding

   1   pound mashed potatoes   1 gill brandy
   ¾ pound butter   1 gill rose water
   ¾ pound sugar   1 gill cream
   7 eggs

Beat the butter and sugar together, the eggs to a froth. Combine ingredients and bake in pudding dish.

Black Cake

- 1 pound of flour
- 1 pound of sugar
- 1 pound of butter
- 2 pounds of currants
- 2 pounds raisins
- 12 eggs beat light
- spice

IPC

Jumbles

- ¾ pound butter
- ¾ pound sugar
- whites of 4 eggs
- 1 pound flour
- nutmeg
- caraway seed

Roll in sugar

Apple Pudding

- 1 quart steamed apples
- ¼ pound butter
- 4 eggs
- grated bread
- nutmeg and rose water

Bake in paste.

Gingerbread

- 2 pounds flour
- ½ pound sugar
- ½ pound butter
- caraway seed
- ginger
- allspice
- orange peel
- pint of molasses

IPC

Baked Pears

Peel 6 large pears, cut in half lengthwise, take out the cores, stick 2 cloves in each half—over the pears pour 3 tablespoons honey and ½ cup water. Bake one hour in very slow oven. Remove cloves, let cool for 15 minutes. Now mix the liquid from the cooked pears with 1 teaspoon lemon juice and ½ cup good Madeira wine. Pour this over the pears. Sprinkle with ground nuts (almonds and pecans) and serve cold with rich cream.

Apple Sauce

Peel and cut up apples, remove cores, put in pot with ½ cup water and boil with lid on till tender. Mash with a potato masher and then add ¼ cup sugar.

Pumpkin Pie

- 1 cup of sugar or to taste
- 8 heaping spoonfuls of strained pumpkin
- 2 eggs beaten slightly
- 1 cup milk
- 1 teaspoon cinnamon
- 1 teaspoon ginger
- 3 tablespoons brandy

ST

Strawberry Delight

Sweeten strawberries and get very cold. Add whipped cream.

Add Kirsch or Benedictine or any sweet liquor. Beat well together with spoon. Not too much cream.

Birds Eye Raspberries with whipped cream, apricot brandy. Mix thoroughly.

Pears Sublime

Peel and core pears and cut in halves. Put a clove in each and place in baking dish and add ½ cup cold water and ½ cup of honey. Bake in slow oven—basting frequently. When done let cool for 20 minutes then put pears in dish they are to be served in—to liquid add ½ cup sherry and one tablespoon of lemon juice and pour over pears. CPR

Rice Pudding

2 tablespoons rice—wash in hot water, leave in pudding dish, add 2½ tablespoons sugar, butter (½ tablespoon) and nutmeg. Stir together. Add 1 quart and 1 pint milk and put in slow oven for several hours, stirring at least six times. Add raisins when half done.

Baked Chocolate Pudding

Melt 3 squares unsweetened chocolate with tablespoon of hot water in double boiler. Add slowly ½ cup sugar and heaping tablespoon flour. Mix well together then pour in ½ cup melted butter and 2 teaspoons vanilla. Remove from fire and add 4 well-beaten egg yolks. Then beat egg whites and fold into mixture. Put in well-buttered china mold and set mold in pan of hot water. Bake in moderate oven for 1 hour. Let cool in mold. Turn into a dessert dish and serve with sauce.

MOCHA CREAM SAUCE
to be served with the above pudding

Beat 2 egg yolks and add ¼ cup sugar, pinch of salt and ½ cup of very strong coffee. Cook in double boiler till thick. When cold fold into a cup of whipped cream. CPR

To Toast Pecans

To one pound shelled nuts add three tablespoons melted butter, two tablespoons Wesson oil, turn about gently. Place in large flat baking pan (biscuit sheet) and put in slow oven until crisp but still light brown, stirring gently frequently. When done place on paper towels, sprinkle with 1 level teaspoon salt, stir gently.

Peach Melba

Cool peach halves. Fill cup with vanilla or burnt almond ice cream. Cover with sweetened crushed raspberries. VP

Indian Muffins

1 quart of meal scalded	1 pint of milk
2 eggs	1 wineglass of yeast
½ pound of wheat flour and a little salt	

Make it a stiff batter so that it will drop from spoon.

Creme Brulee

Boil one pint of thick cream for one minute. Pour it on the well-beaten yolks of four eggs. Place it on the fire and allow it gradually to come almost to the boiling point. Pour the mixture into dish in which it is to be served—allow it to get cold—then strew over the top a layer of brown sugar. Place in a slow oven for 10 minutes, then brown quickly with a salamander and serve cold.

Serve coffee ice cream with Creme de Cocoa

Casserole of Apples

Pare and core 5 apples and cut in thin slices. Place layer of apples in buttered casserole. Add layer red currant jelly—continue adding layer upon layer ending with apple layer. Cover and bake in very hot oven until apples are soft. Uncover and sprinkle with 3 tablespoons granulated sugar and cinnamon—put under broiler to caramel and serve with rum custard sauce.

Rum Custard Sauce for above Casserole

1 tablespoon sugar
1 egg
thin cream and rum

CPR

Chocolate Ice Box Pudding

- 1½ packages German Sweet Chocolate
- 2 dozen lady fingers
- 6 eggs
- 1 scant cup water

Put chocolate in water in double boiler. When melted add egg yolks, beaten separately and to which one tablespoon of sugar has been added. Cook 3 minutes. Remove from fire and add beaten egg whites to which 1 cup sugar has been added. Put wax paper in mould and line with lady fingers. Pour in mixture, placing remaining lady fingers in center. Let stand over night in ice box or make early in AM for dinner.   CPR

Sweet Potato Pudding

5 large tablespoonsful of grated potato, 1 quart of boiling milk, 5 eggs, and 5 tablespoonsful of sugar, 1 tablespoonful of rose water, and half a nutmeg, and a piece of butter the size of an egg. Pour the milk on the potato, then beat the eggs well with the sugar, and after adding the other ingredients, bake it.

MEMORANDA

MEMORANDA

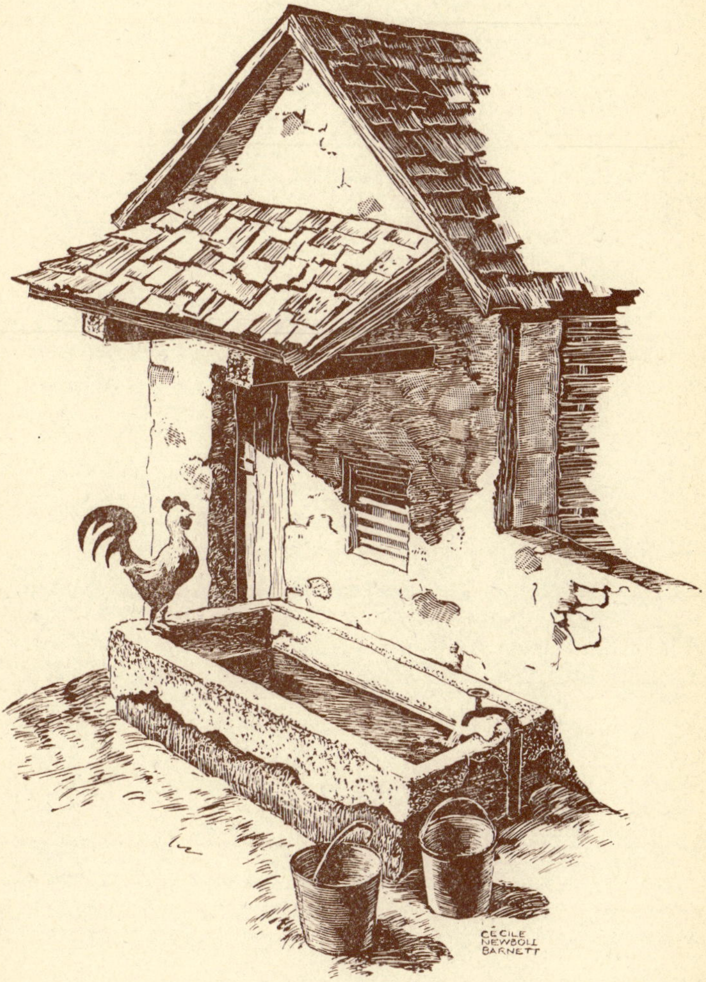
CÉCILE
NEWBOLD
BARNETT

BEVERAGES

May Wine

   1 ounce dried woodruff or waldmeister
  10 bottles chilled white wine
     (Moselle, Riesling or Rhine)
   1 bottle chilled Champagne
   2 ounces Benedictine
   2 ounces Cognac
   ¼ pound granulated sugar
   1 quart sparkling water

Place ice in jug inside punch bowl

Steep woodruff for six hours in one bottle white wine.

Place mixture in punch bowl, stir and add remaining white wine. Add Champagne, Benedictine and Cognac. Stir. Add sparkling water. Drop in fresh strawberries and garnish with bits of fresh woodruff.

Grape Juice

Weigh 10 pounds of grapes (stemmed)
Add 3 pints of water and cook until tender, pour in jelly bag and drain. To this juice add three pounds of sugar. Let come to a boil and bottle and seal. Water can be added when opened.

AUNT FH

Kentucky Mint Ice-Tea Syrup

    2 cups water   grated rind of 3 lemons
    1 cup sugar   2 cups mint (whole)

Boil syrup 5 minutes—pour hot syrup over mint leaves and grated lemon rind. Cover and stand overnight. Next morning pour through strainer, squeezing leaves to extract all juice; add juice from the 3 lemons. Add to cold tea approximately ⅓ syrup to ⅔ cold tea. Decorate glasses with sprig of mint.

vw

Syllabubs

Put into a large punchbowl a bottle of wine, sweeten it to your palate, and grate in the third part of a nutmeg; stir this about, and then take it to the cow; let there be milked into it as much as will make a proper quantity of syllabub, then pour upon it half a pint of rich cream. This is the common syllabub, to which the cream is a very great addition. It may be made with cyder as well as wine, and may be prepared at home in this manner. Put the wine, sugar, and nutmeg together, and have the cream ready; make a sufficient quantity of milk, that is about a quart, as warm as when it comes from the cow, put it into a large teapot, and pour it into the bowl to the wine; hold the teapot at a considerable height above the bowl, and it will do as well as milking the cow.

Wine Bitters

Take ¼ pound of gentian, ¼ pound bitter orange peel, 3 drams cochineal, to 1 gallon brandy. Pound the cochineal.

Pineapple Punch

    1 large can pineapple juice
    1 pint cold black tea
    ⅓ cup lemon juice

Strain over ice and just before serving add 2 bottles ginger ale or soda water

vp

Everlasting Syllabubs

This is a sort of whipped syllabub, that will keep a week or ten days, and be all the while as good as first; and it is a very rich and well-tasted kind. Put into a very large bowl half a pint of sack, and the same quantity of Rhenish; squeeze in three large seville oranges, and add a pound of the finest sugar beaten to powder; stir these well together; then grate in the fine upper yellow part of two large lemons; stir it once again together, and then pour in a quart and half a pint of rich cream; beat it about with a whisk for an hour, or mill it with a chocolate mill, which is the best way, and when it is well frothed put in one spoonful of orange-flower water; beat it up again and when it is enough fill the glasses with a clean silver spoon.

After a severe illness, a syllabub has been found stimulating to the appetite.

Egg-Nog

To yolks of 18 eggs use 3 pints best bourbon whiskey, 3 quarts heavy cream and about 1½ pints of granulated sugar with a grating of nutmeg. First, if the egg-nog is to be served at four or a little later, put the whiskey and sugar together at 9 A M and let stand for 3 hours. Have ready yolks beaten to a light froth, drop the eggs a little at a time stirring constantly to keep from curdling. When it is perfectly smooth cover the bowl and let stand for 2½ hours. Have ready cream whipped well and add it to the whiskey and egg yolks. Pack bowl in ice for an hour or more and it is ready to serve. Never use white of eggs. The mixing is the main thing—if not strong enough add more whiskey after it is mixed.

Serves 30 or 40 people.

Holiday Cocktail

1 part lemon juice
2 parts apricot brandy
3 parts Rum (Jamaica)
Shake very well till very cold.

Whip Syllabub

Take half a pint of wine, 2 lemons, loaf sugar enough to sweeten it, whites of 3 eggs beat to a froth, add one quart of cream. You may add any of the ingredients till agreeable to your taste.

Planters Punch

  1 sour   3 strong
  2 sweet   4 weak

Claret Cup

To 1 quart claret, add one pint of water, 2 oranges sliced, 2 lemons sliced, and one lemon squeezed. Sugar to taste. 2 wine glasses of brandy and one of cordial, or three of cordial and no brandy.

One Gallon Pitcher

  3½ quarts home made claret
  1   tumbler lemon juice
  1   pint Jamaica Rum
  3   tablespoons granulated sugar (or more if desired)
      Add sliced oranges if desired

One gallon is ample for 24 to 30 people

Spiritual Facts

That whiskey is the key by which many gain entrance into our prisins and almhouses
That brandy brands the noses of all those who cannot govern their appetites
That punch is the cause of many unfriendly punches
That ale causes many ailings, while beer brings to the bier
That wine causes many to take a winding way home
That champagne is the source of many real pains.
That gin slings have slewed more than slings of oil

Mint Julep

3, 4, or 6 sprigs of mint (well toasted)
½ glass of crushed ice

Fill glass with water ¾ full, 2 heaping spoonsful sugar and fill with whiskey or brandy.

Cocktail Schaw

½ Cognac
¼ Vermouth Francais
¼ Gr Mariner

Restaurant de L'Escargot
38 Rue Montorgueil, Paris

MEMORANDA

MEMORANDA

MEMORANDA

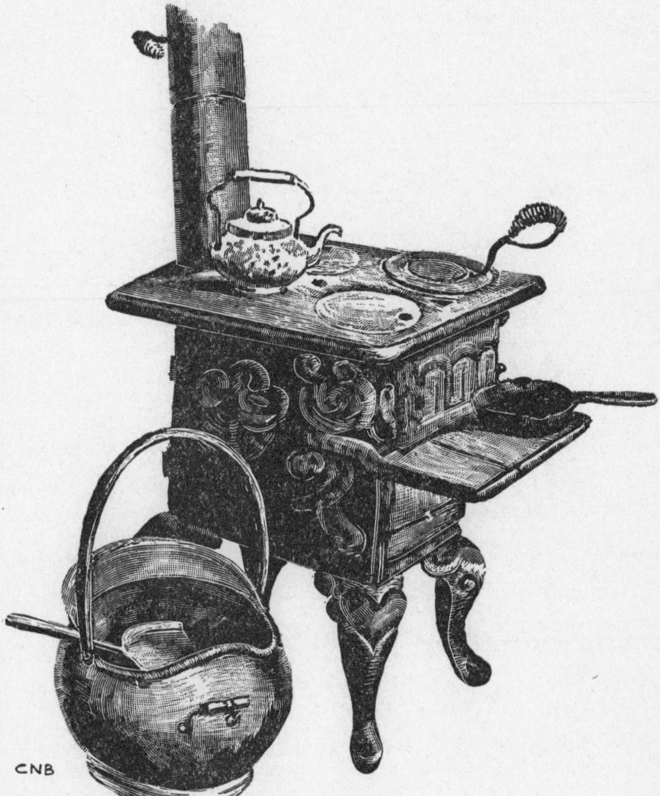
CNB

PRESERVES

Spiced Watermelon

Pare the green rind off the watermelon, cut the white part into one inch squares, put on in cold water and boil slowly until the sections can be easily pierced with a fork.

½ pint of vinegar and 1 pound of sugar to each pound of rind, weighed before boiling.

Boil the sugar and vinegar and whole spices (cinnamon, cloves and mace) and pour *hot* over rind which has been placed in a bowl or crock. Repeat this every day or every other day until the syrup is thick as honey and clear. Always pour the syrup hot over the rind.   MRS. PC

Chili Sauce—100 years old

- 12 tomatoes—peeled
- 4 large onions ⎫
- 3 peppers ⎭ —chopped fine
- 1 teaspoon cloves
- 1 teaspoon allspice
- 1 teaspoon ginger
- ½ cup sugar
- 2 teaspoons salt
- 1 pint vinegar

Cook one hour and bottle while hot.   FR

Herbs

The herbs used as seasoning are parsley, mint, sage, thyme, marjoram and winter savory. These, of course, can be used in the fresh condition, but it is useful in wintertime to have a store of dried herbs.

The herbs should be gathered just when the young plants are about to flower, and, if possible, when they are dry and not exposed to strong sunshine. Small-leaved herbs such as thyme and winter savory should be washed, tied in bundles, protected from dust with a piece of muslin and hung up to dry near the kitchen fire. With the large-leaved herbs the leaves should be picked from the stalks, any shrivelled ones being discarded. The leaves should be tied in muslin and dipped in boiling water, removed, superfluous water shaken off and placed in a cool oven at a temperature between 110° F and 130° F. The leaves should be dried until they are quite crisp. If the drying process can be carried out continuously, it takes one hour, but if the leaves are placed on the rack above the stove, it takes from three to four hours. When dry, the herbs should be crushed with a rolling pin and sieved to a fine powder, which should be stored in bottles and protected from the light. Small-leaved herbs should also be crushed and sieved, and stored as above.

Spiced Peaches

1 peck of hard peaches
4 cups sugar
2 cups strong cider vinegar
1 tablespoon whole cloves
1 tablespoon whole allspice
1 teaspoon mace
6 inch piece of stick cinnamon

Put the sugar, vinegar, spices, and 2 cups of water into preserving kettle; boil 10 minutes, then add the peaches which have been washed, pared and cut in half. Boil slowly 30 minutes; remove all scum; put the peaches into sterilised jars and cover with the syrup. If the syrup seems too thin let it boil 15 minutes longer. Be sure that the jars do not leak—when cold put into a cool, dark place.

JJ

Dried Fruits and Vegetables

Vegetables should be young and fresh. Before drying, most vegetables are blanched either by steaming for 5 to 10 minutes or by putting in boiling salted water for about 5 minutes. Boiled vegetables should be put in cold water and well drained before being spread on trays for drying.

Dried beans and peas are useful and nutritious, particularly for use in Winter, when fresh vegetables are scarce. Any variety of peas can be dried if there is a surplus, but if grown specially for drying, it is advisable to choose particular varieties. The pods should be allowed to ripen on the plants, and the seeds then removed from the pods and stored in any dry container. If the weather is bad, it may be advisable to dry the pods under cover, and the whole plants should then be lifted, tied in bundles and hung up to dry in any airy place. Before using the beans or peas, they should be soaked for 24 hours.

The fruit or vegetables should be allowed to cool for 12 hours before they are packed away. During this time they should be covered with paper or cheese cloth to protect them from insects. When thoroughly cool they may be packed in paper bags or in jars or tins, but must be kept in a dry place. They should be inspected from time to time, but if sufficiently dried they should keep perfectly.

Bouquet Garni

A bouquet garni is merely a mixture of various herbs that go well together, in specific proportions. For soups and stews in the following proportions: 1 tablespoon each thyme, marjoram, dried parsley, sage, grated dried lemon rind, celery seed, and six bay leaves. Or a few celery tops, leeks, parsley, one bay leaf, two cloves, thyme, one clove garlic. Place in cheesecloth bag and remove when desired flavor is achieved. Or fresh, in cheesecloth bag, few sprigs parsley, marjoram, tarragon, thyme, two bay leaves. Or one teaspoon dried parsley, marjoram, thyme, one-fourth teaspoon dried sage, two teaspoons dried celery tops.

Peaches and Pears

After paring and coring, put amongst them sufficient sugar to make them palatable for present eating,—about 3 to 4 lbs only for each bushel; let them heat to a boil, and continue the boiling, with care, from 20 to 30 minutes; or sufficiently long to heat through, which expels the air.

Canning

Have ready a kettle of hot water, into which dip the can long enough to heat it; then fill in the fruit while hot, corking it immediately, and dip the end of the cork into the "Cement for Canning Fruits." When cold it is best to dip the second time to make sure that no air holes are left which would spoil the fruit. All canned fruits are to be kept in a very cool, dark cellar.

Berries, Plums, Cherries

Raspberries, blackberries, whortleberries currants, cherries, and plums, need not be boiled over 10 to 15 minutes; using sugar to make platable, in all cases; as it must be put in some time, and it helps to preserve the fruit.

They require the same care in heating cans as the above for peaches.

Tomatoes

For tomatoes, scald and peel them as for other cooking; then scald, or rather boil for about 15 minutes only, and can as above.

What is best, is to use a little salt, and put them into half-gallon jugs; for we want them in too great quantities to stop on a few glass jars, such as we use for other fruits; as for tin cans, never use them. If you do use tin cans for tomatoes it will not do to use salt with them, as it has a tendency to cause rust.

Strawberries

For strawberries, put sugar ½ lb. for each lb. of berries; and proceed as for Berries.

Strawberries are so juicy, and have such a tendency to fermentation, that it is almost impossible to keep them unless you adopt the plan of using the amount of sugar above named.

Salting of Beans

For every 3 or 4 pounds beans, 1 pound salt will be required. Failures are often due to the use of too little salt. The beans should be young, fresh and tender. Wash, dry, remove strings and slice the beans, or if very small leave whole. Place a layer of salt in a stoneware jar and on this a layer of sliced beans. Continue to fill the jar with alternate layers, pressing the beans down well, and finishing with a layer of salt. Cover and leave for a few days. The beans shrink, and the jar should then be filled up with more beans and salt. The salt does not remain dry, as it draws moisture from the beans and forms a strong brine. When full, cork the jar securely, and paint over the cork with melted paraffin. To use, remove them from salt, wash thoroughly in several waters, then soak for 2 hours in warm water. They get tough if soaked overnight. Cook in boiling water without salt, until they are tender. Drain and serve in the same way as fresh runner beans.

Green Tomato Mince Meat

1 peck green tomatoes
½ peck apples
2 packages raisins
5 pounds brown sugar
3 teaspoons cloves
1 tablespoon nutmeg
1 cup vinegar
1 pound suet
3 lemons, cut up fine

Put tomatoes through chopper and let stand an hour. Measure and put same quantity of hot water with tablespoon salt. Boil five minutes, then drain two hours. Put all together and boil one hour. Put in jars.

MRS. L

Brine Pickles that will Remain Hard

Pick the cucumbers and wash; put them in your jar or keg and cover with coarse salt. Next day put in your next picking and cover with salt and so on till the jar is filled; do not add water as the moisture from the cucumbers is enough to wet the salt. When you freshen them cover with the following: To every quart of vinegar add 1½ cups white sugar and level teaspoonful cinnamon and cayenne pepper the size of a pea. Heat and pour over the pickles. Good as soon as cold.   IPC

Spiced Peaches or Seckle Pears

    7 pounds of fruit
    3 pounds sugar
    1 pint of vinegar

Whole spices, as much as you like. We use stick cinnamon and about one dozen cloves. Pare fruit and heat the syrup, pour over fruit and let stand over night. In morning boil till fruit is tender and then put in jars and seal.   MRS. HB

Good Grape Jelly

Stem and wash the grapes and cook slowly without water, stirring frequently. Drain through a jelly bag. Add an equal portion of heated sugar to the boiling juice and boil 20 minutes.   MRS. MB

Peach and Orange Marmalade

Grind up together 12 peaches and 2 oranges and cook for 40 minutes with an equal amount of sugar. Stir frequently to prevent burning.   MRS. MB

Parsley

If parsley is placed in a very hot oven for one minute, it will be found that the colour is very much better than if it is dried by the slower method. Care must be taken to avoid scorching.

Tomato Catsup—Wilson Rule-1884

- 1 peck tomatoes
- 1 pint cider vinegar
- ¼ cup salt
- ½ oz black pepper
- ¼ oz cayenne
- ½ oz whole allspice
- a few cloves
- 10 pods garlic
- ¼ oz best mustard
- 2 large onions minced fine
- ½ pound brown sugar
- handful peach leaves

Boil mass for 3 hours. Stir to prevent burning. When cold, strain and seal. It will improve with age and will create an appetite almost under the ribs of death.   MM

Easy to Make Grape Butter

- 1 quart of grapes
- ¾ quart of sugar

Boil 20 minutes, then put through a sieve and then into jelly glasses or jars.   MRS. RK

Peach Marmalade

To 10 peaches take 1 orange and 1 lemon and 2 peach kernels mashed. Put oranges and lemons through meat chopper. To every cup of the mixture add scant ¾ cup sugar. Boil 40 minutes, stirring constantly.

Mrs. Brown's Chutney Sauce

- 2 quarts green or ripe tomatoes
- 12 large sour apples
- 4 red peppers
- 8 small onions
- 1 quart vinegar
- 2 pounds sugar
- 1¼ pounds raisins
- 2 tablespoons white mustard
- 1 tablespoon cinnamon
- 1 tablespoon allspice
- 2 tablespoons salt
- 1 teaspoon cloves

Mix ingredients in order given and cook slowly four hours, stirring often to prevent scorching, and until thick consistency.   EH

Grape Catsup

- 9 pounds strained grapes
- 5 pounds sugar
- 2 tablespoons cinnamon, allspice, cloves and
- ¼ teaspoon red pepper

Boil mixture until thick and when cool thin with vinegar.

FBY

Hawaiian Jam

- 6 pounds Concord grapes
- 5 pounds sugar
- 1 pound seeded raisins
- 4 large oranges
- 1 cup chopped nuts

Wash grapes, separate skins and pulp. Cook pulp 15 minutes, press through sieve to remove seeds. Add pulp to skins, add sugar, raisins, and the juice and chopped rinds of oranges. Boil 20 minutes. Mix well; add nuts and cook 5 minutes.

FBY

Cranberry Jelly

Boil 1 quart cranberries and 1 cup of water in covered pan for 5 or 6 minutes—press through sieve—stir in two cups of sugar until melted. Pour into molds and set aside until wanted. DO NOT BOIL AFTER ADDING SUGAR. This never fails and is so easy to make.

MHC

Warners Gout Cordial

Rhubarb 1 ounce
Senna 2 drams
Coriander and fennel seed each 1 dram
Saffron, Liquorice root and Cochineal of each ½ dram
Raisins sliced and stoned, half a pound infused in a quart of brandy for 10 days. Strain it off and add 1 pint brandy to the same ingredients. Let it remain until the virtue is quite extracted, then mix the pint and quart together. A tablespoonful to be taken in the same quantity of boiling water and repeat the dose if the pain does not abate.

Japonica Jelly

Wash fruit—quarter it without paring. Remove cores. Put in sauce pan, cover with water, and bring rapidly to boil and cook until fruit is tender. Strain through jelly bag. Measure juice. Bring it to a boil and add 1 scant cup of sugar to each cup of juice. Let it boil rapidly until it will jelly drop. Remove from fire, let it stand a moment then skim top. Pour in glasses and let cool. Cover with wax. Very good served with pork. EBT

Pear Marmalade

6 pounds Keiffer pears
6 oranges
2 lemons or 1 grapefruit
6 pounds sugar

Peel pears and remove cores. Grind all the fruits together in good grinder. Add sugar and cook all together until thick. Let cool, then seal in jars. EBT

Pepper Relish

18 large green peppers
18 large red peppers
18 large onions
3 pints vinegar
3 tbs celery seed
3 tbs mustard seed
4 cups sugar

Grind peppers and onions in food chopper. Add 1 cup salt and let stand 15 minutes. Scald and drain three times with boiling water. Add vinegar and spices and sugar. Cook all together 20 minutes, and seal in pint jars. EBT

Preserved Apples

Pare and halve them. Take 1 pound sugar to 1 pound apples. 1 quart water to 4 pounds sugar. Boil them slow. Boil the lemon peel, change the water three times. Then cut it small. Put some liquor of the last boiling into the syrup after the apples are taken up—boil it up—while it is boiling put the lemon peel in.

Apple Chutney

- 12 green apples
- 1 onion
- 3 peppers (2 green, 1 red)
- 1 cup seeded and chopped raisins
- 1 pint cider vinegar
- ½ cup currant jelly
- 2 cups sugar
- juice of four lemons
- 1 tablespoon ground ginger
- 1 tablespoon salt
- ¼ tablespoon cayenne

Chop apples, onion, and peppers very fine. Add vinegar and jelly. Let simmer one hour, stirring often. Add other ingredients and cook another hour, stirring constantly. Put in jars and seal. ABH

Cucumber Relish

- 2 quarts cucumbers
- 2 tablespoons salt—let stand one hour—drain

Add 2 cups sugar   2 onions sliced
2 cups vinegar   2 teaspoons mixed spice

Boil for 5 minutes
Fill jars and seal
Add green pepper if desired. ABH

Candied Orange or Grapefruit Peel

Peel in quarters or halves orange peel and grapefruit rind. Soak in salt water overnight. Boil off three times until bitterness disappears and until rind is tender. Scoop out as much of white pulp as possible. Cut orange peel or grapefruit rind in thin strips. Boil in syrup of 1 cup of sugar, ½ cup of water until clear and crystal. Dip in pulverized sugar and lay on plate to dry overnight. Keep in cracker jar. EMT

Tomato Ketchup

1 gallon of skinned tomatoes
4 tablespoons salt
4 teaspoons black pepper
½ teaspoon allspice
8 pods red pepper
8 tablespoons mustard

Articles ground fine and simmered slowly in sharp vinegar, in a pewter basin 3 or 4 hours and then strained through a wire sieve and bottled close. It may be used in 2 weeks, but improves much by age. Those who like the article may add, after the simmering is over and the ingredients somewhat cooled, 2 tablespoons of the juice of garlic. So much vinegar is to be used as to have ½ gallon of liquor when the process is over. To my taste this is superior to any West India ketchup that I ever met with and it is withal an excellent remedy for dispepsia.

Pickle for Beef or Pork (Knickerbocker)

Take 6 gallons of water, 9 pounds of salt, half coarse and half fine, 3 pounds coarse brown sugar, 1 quart of molasses, 3 ounces saltpetre, 1 ounce pearlash. These ingredients form the pickle, which must be well boiled and carefully skimmed and when quite cold poured over the beef or pork previously placed into the tub or barrel; then cover your barrel closely to keep out all dust. The pickle should be sufficient to cover the beef or pork. The above ingredients will make sufficient pickle for 100 pounds of pork.

Pickled Oysters

After they are opened wash them clean in their own liquor then scald them in it after pouring it clear—take them out and spread them on cloths to dry and cool. Strain the liquor and to every two quarts of liquor add one quart of good vinegar, a handful of whole pepper and a handful of salt, a handful of allspice, a little mace. Boil it well and skim it—take it off to cool—put the oysters in pots and to every layer of oysters one of spice and fill them up with liquor. Tie them down close.

To Pickle Tomatoes

Take a peck of tomatoes, stem them and pick them five or six times with a fork. Pack them in 2 quarts of salt or more if you think they require it. Let them lay eight days; then let them lay two days in cold vinegar and water. Slice 6 onions, a bottle of mustard, cloves and red or black pepper to taste. Place them in layers with the onions, etc. between. Pour cold vinegar over them. In ten days they will be fit for use.

Calves Feet Jelly

Boil four feet in four quarts of water until half is boiled away, then pour it in a pan to cool. When perfectly cold, take the top off, then the jelly must be carefully removed from any sediment that may be in the bottom, put the jelly into a Bell metal kettle and let it warm; then add loaf sugar to your taste, say one pound or more, two gills of wine, the juice of three lemons, the skin of one and two or three sticks of cinnamon. Boil for fifteen minutes, then set it off the fire until nearly cool, beat the whites of 5 eggs, and shells and pour into it, then let it boil 20 minutes without stirring, strain it through a flannel bag until clear; scald the bag first to prevent waste. Beef feet will make jelly by the same process, taking two feet instead of four. IPC

Cedar Syrup

Take the green parts of cedar bushes and the young twigs and put them in a kettle with sufficient water to cover them. Boil them about a hour or till the strength appears to be extracted. Take them out and put in another portion of the cedar bushes to the same tea and boil them the same. Strain the tea through a piece of muslin or a fine hair sieve and to 2 quarts of the cedar tea put one pint of honey, ½ pound rock candy, ½ pound of loaf sugar, ¼ pound of liquorice and ounce of gum arabic. Boil them a half hour. When cold take a wine glassful 3 times a day. The syrup should be kept in a cool place as it is liable to ferment. IPC

Pepper Hash

    12 onions
    12 red peppers
    12 green peppers

Remove seeds of all but 8
Wash and chop
Pour boiling water over onions and peppers
Let stand 5 minutes. Then drain in a colander. Then add 2 pints vinegar.
    2½ tablespoons salt
    2 cups sugar
Boil together for 10 minutes.
Put into jars while hot.
MRS. L

Lavender Compound

To 1 pint lavender spirits, 12 cloves, peel of 1 orange, ½ dram english saffron, ½ dram cochineal, 1 ounce cinnamon

Currant Jelly

1 pound of sugar to one pint juice. Let it boil exactly 15 minutes. If longer it will candy.
IPC

Blackberry Jam

To 10 pounds of fruit, 6 pounds sugar, then boil it until it looks rich.

Quince Marmalade

12 pounds of quinces to 6 pounds sugar, boil the quinces in a little water until they are soft, mash them through a sieve. Put the sugar to the water in which they are boiled. Clarify it, then put in the pulp and boil it until stiff.

NB—I generally mash them through a colander.
AJC

Cider Vinegar

As there are those who will not have any but cider vinegar, and have plenty of cider out of which to make it, this will give you the best plan of proceeding for manufacturers:

Have a room where it will not freeze; place on end as many barrels or large casks, without heads, to hold as much as you wish to make; fill these one-third full of soft water, and the other two-thirds with apple cider; yeast 2 quarts to each cask.

In a few weeks you will have good vinegar; without the yeast it would be all the season in becoming good. Then fill up into barrels for sale, leaving a little, say one-eighth, in the open barrels, and fill them up with water and cider as before, and it will become good much quicker than before. If the water is objected to, use the cider without it, but pure cider makes vinegar too strong for any one to use, and requires much longer time in making. These barrels may have boards over them to keep out flies and dirt. If the retainer can give it his attention, by having a barrel of good cider vinegar to sell out of, he can always keep it up, if, when he draws out two or three gallons of the vinegar, he will go to his cider; kept for the purpose, and replace the vinegar with the cider; or if making with molasses and water or any other article, fill up with the same; but take notice, if you forget or neglect, and draw your vinegar nearly all out before you fill in, it does not keep to the point sharpness desired, unless you have two or three barrels.

To Pickle Plums or Cherries

To seven pounds of fruit take three pounds of brown sugar, 1 ounce of cloves and 1 ounce of mace, 1 quart of vinegar. Mix the sugar and vinegar, boil and skim it then add the spice; pour it boiling hot over the fruit and let it stand 24 hours. Repeat the boiling 8 or 9 times or till the fruit is perfectly cooked. Cherries do not require to be put over the fire but plums ought to be the last time the syrup is boiled. IPC

Butter—

To Preserve Any Length of Time

First—work out all the buttermilk. Second—use rock salt. Third—pack in air-tight jars or cans. Fourth—keep in a cool place, and you will have nice butter for years, if desired to keep so long. A short recipe, but it makes long butter.

Merchants, who take in more butter than they can sell during the warm months, can put it into jars and cover the jar with about half an inch of lard over the top of the butter, and place it in the cellar; or they can put about an inch or two of brine in place of the lard, and have it do well, first working out all the buttermilk which may remain, when bought in. It would be well for them to have their regular customers to furnish them butter, to whom they furnish the right kind of salt, as the rock, or crystal salt, does not contain so much lime as the common, which is evaporated by artificial heat. Let sugar, and saltpeter, and all other peters, alone, if you wish good butter, either for present use or long keeping.

Mrs. Ryan's Grape Jam

Wash and stem Concord grapes. Measure equal parts of grapes and sugar. Bring to boil. Boil 20 minutes. Put through sieve and seal.

JR

Tomato Mustard

Take a peck of tomatoes and cut them in slices and put them in an earthen jar. Let them boil until quite soft then put them through a sieve; till nothing remains but the skin and seed, then put the pulp again in the pot, let it boil until quite thick and the liquor almost gone, then take one tablespoonful of red pepper, one of black, one of cloves, one of allspice, two of mustard seed, one of mace (all ground fine) four spoonfuls of salt. Let it boil up, then put it into jars, and tie it up from the air.

Lemon Butter

Grated rind and juice of two lemons, 2 beaten eggs, 1½ cups sugar and small piece of butter, about the size of a walnut. Let boil up once. Must be stirred constantly.   EBT

MEMORANDA

MEMORANDA

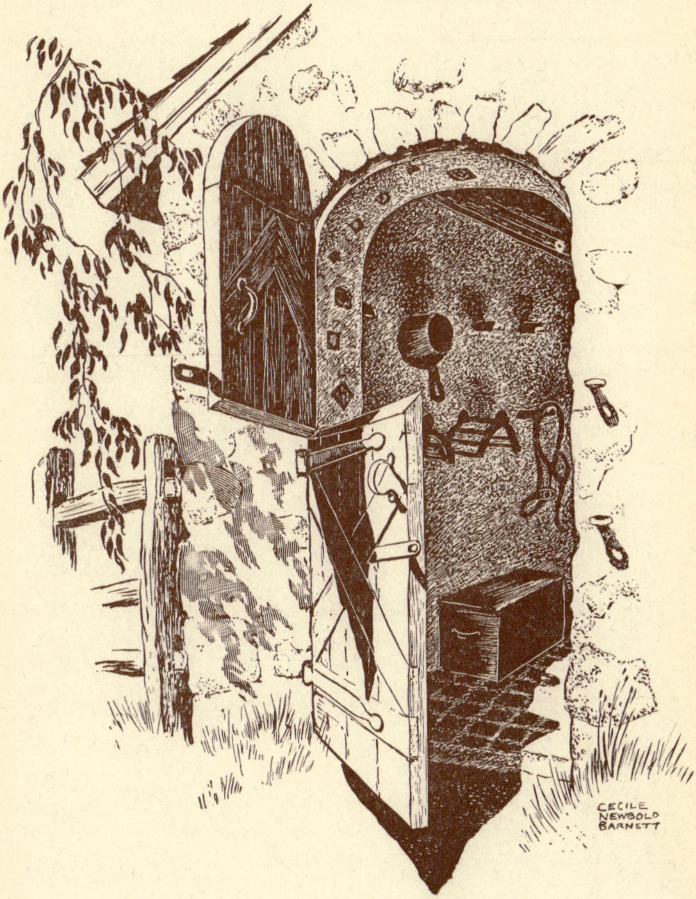
CECILE
NEWBOLD
BARNETT

MISCELLANEOUS

Fruits to Keep—

Without Loss of Color or Flavor
To each pound of rosin, put 1 oz. of tallow, and 1 oz. of beeswax. Melt them slowly over the fire in an iron kettle, and be careful and not let it boil. Take the fruit separately and rub it over the whiting or fine chalk (to prevent the coating from adhering to the fruit). Then dip it into the solution once and hold it up a moment to set the coating; then pack away carefully in barrels or boxes in a cool place. When you dip oranges or lemons, loop a thread around to hold them; for pears or apples, insert a pointed stick to hold them by, then cut it off with a pair of sharp, heavy shears. Oranges or lemons cannot be put in boxes but must be placed on shelves, as the accumulated weight would mash them down.

To Make Baking Powder

1 pound cream tartar
½ pound soda
1 cup corn starch.

Sift all together ten or 12 times.

EH

Eggs—

To Preserve For Winter Use

For every three gallons of water put in 1 pt. of fresh slacked lime, and common salt 1-2 pt.; mix well, and let the barrel be about half full of this fluid, then with a dish let down your fresh eggs into it, tipping the dish after it fills with water, so they roll out without cracking the shell, for if the shell is cracked the egg will spoil.

If fresh eggs are put in fresh eggs will come out. A piece of board may be laid across the top of the eggs, and a little lime and salt kept upon it, which keeps the fluid as strong at the top as at the bottom. This will not fail you. They must always be kept covered with the brine. Families in towns and cities by this plan can have eggs for winter use at summer prices.

Rosemary

Tuck bits under skin of roast lamb or chops while cooking.

Harvest herbs before they flower—dry between August 15 and Sept. 15

Lemon Verbena makes excellent tea—simmer 3 minutes. Leave in cellar over winter

Caraway seeds in small bag in water to boil new potatoes—add dill instead of parsley

Chervil grown in shade

Omelets with parsley and chives

Add honey to French dressing

Cheese herbs
    Fennel seeds crushed
    Annis seeds crushed
    Tarragon
    Chervil
    Dried chives

Top cream cheese with herbs

To Make a Ham

Cut off a fine large ham from the hind quarter of a good sizeable hog; grind an ounce of salt petre in a marble mortar, put to it a pound of common salt, and a pound of coarse sugar; rub them well together, and cover the ham with this, working it well in; lay it in a large pan and pour the rest of the mixture over it; this will melt into a fine pickle; let the ham be turned in it every day, and well basted with it; let it lie thus a month, and then be hung up in a place where there comes wood smoak, and where there is little heat; when it is thoroughly dried it is fit for use; but it will keep a long time, and when there is opportunity, it is best to give them a sort of preparation, by hanging them in a damper place before they are dressed, for a month; this will take a great effect upon the flesh, making it excellently tender; if they grow a little mouldy in this hanging, it is so much the better, for they will not be tainted on the inside though covered with it.

To Make Bacon

Cut off all the inside fat from a side of a hog; lay in on a dresser, and let it lie for the blood to run away; then salt it carefully and thoroughly on both sides with common salt, rubbing it well in; let it lie thus a week, then beat in a marble mortar a quarter of a pound of salt petre, add to this a pint of bay salt, beat them together pretty fine, add a quarter of a peck of common salt, and grind this well with them; then put in two pounds of coarse sugar; lay the side in a shallow trough, and rub in this mixture as you did the salt, that it may penetrate and cover every part; lay the outside downward in the trough. These ingredients will melt and make a great deal of pickle; let this be poured upon the side every day for a fortnight; it is then preserved but wants drying; let it be hung up in a place where wood is burnt, and when it is well dryed keep it in a dry place. The best manner of preserving it is to hang it up from the ceiling, that the air may come freely to it every way; and let the place be airy, but not hot; hanging against anything always spoils bacon; and heat makes it rusty.

To Make Yeast

Grate large raw potato. Add 1 tablespoon flour and stir till smooth. Add boiling water till like cream. ½ cup sugar, ¼ cup salt, about 1 cup hop tea (made by steeping pinch of hops with cold water on back of stove for 2 hours). Cool and add 1 cake yeast or 1 cup yeast. Set back of stove to rise for 2 days or more. When settled put in jars in cool place. EH

Jug Yeast

without yeast to start with—hops ½ pound; water 1 gallon; fine malt flour ½ pint; brown sugar ½ pound.

Boil the hops in the water until quite strong, strain and stir in the malt flour; and strain again through a coarse cloth, and boil again for ten minutes; when lukewarm, stir in the sugar, and place in a jug, keeping it at the same temperature until it works over; when cork tight, and keep in a cold place.

Sandwiches

Equal parts of chopped nuts and chopped seedless raisins. Moisten with mayonnaise. A few drops of lemon juice. Spread generously between thin slices of bread. BP

Ground cooked ham. Small amount of finely chopped sweet pickles. Taste that it may not be too acid but nicely flavored. Moisten to spread with mayonnaise. BP

Cocoanut Cream Candy

1½ cups sugar
½ cup milk
2 teaspoons butter
½ cup shredded cocoanut
½ teaspoon vanilla

Melt butter in pan, add sugar and milk, stir till sugar is dissolved, heat to boiling point and cook about 12 minutes, remove from fire, add cocoanut and vanilla, beat until it creams, pour out and cut in squares. CM

Peppermint Drops

Take three pounds of granulated sugar, enough water to melt the sugar. Boil until it ropes; stir or beat until it becomes creamy; add oil of peppermint, making them quite strong of the mint. Drop quickly on light brown paper.　　LBM

Sugared Pop Corn

   1 tablespoon butter
   3 tablespoons water
   1 cup pulverized sugar

Boil till ready to candy, then throw in 3 quarts pop corn. Stir till mixed, take from stove and stir till cool.

Fudge

   1 pound confectioner's sugar　　1/4 pound bitter chocolate
   3 tablespoons cream or milk　　3 tablespoons butter
   1 egg separated　　1 teaspoon vanilla

Mix sugar and butter, add egg yolk. Stir well. Melt chocolate and butter. Add to mixture. Beat egg white to a stiff froth and add vanilla. Beat well together and spread in buttered pan. Cut in squares when hard.　　MRS. HST

Soft Caramels

   1/4 pound of chocolate　　a piece of butter size of a walnut
   1 1/2 pounds brown sugar　　1 teaspoonful flavoring
   1 1/2 cups of cream

Hard Caramels

   1 cake of Baker's chocolate　　1 tablespoon of butter
   3 pounds of coffee sugar　　flavor with vanilla
   1 cup of cream

Cook one-half hour

Sugar Caramels

    3 cups of white sugar
    1 cup of milk
a piece of butter the size of a walnut
    ¼ pound chocolate grated fine

Sugar Nut Candy

12 butternuts chopped in small pieces
½ pound brown sugar
½ cup water

After about 20 minutes on the stove, pour in a buttered china dish

How to Give Children Castor Oil

Take one cup milk, one cup molasses, half cup sugar, half cup castor oil, teaspoonful carbonate of soda, 2 teaspoons ginger, a little salt and enough flour to make a stiff paste. Roll out, cut into shapes and bake in quick oven. One or two as good as a dose of oil.   VP

For a Disordered Stomach

Take dandelions, both roots and leaves and pound them and strain the juice through a rag and take a tablespoonful in the morning, fasting.

For a Cough

    1 ounce liquorice root   1 tablespoon of flaxseed
    1 ounce sugar candy   1 pint water

Stew together and add the juice of one lemon.

When the legs are swelled with dropsy apply lots of wool carded. Bind it around the leg. Tis said it will extract the water.

To Cure a Cough

One ounce Jesuits bark; 1 ounce wild cherry bark; 1 ounce Columba root. Bruise them and put them in a bottle, add one pint of brandy and one quart of water. Take 3 wine glasses full daily or so much as may by experience appear necessary. The above ingredients or barks will bear a repetition of half the quantity of brandy and water.

For a Cancer

Or Hard Tumor in any Part of the Body
Drink plentifully of narrow dock root decoction and it is said that to cut a cranberry in two and bind on the part frequently changing it has been found very efficacious. Poke or Pigeon berry juice is also good to apply to a cancer and has in several instances made a cure. IPC

Cholera Morbus

Tea—to be made of the common oats, such as is used for horses. Simply pouring boiling water on the oats and letting it stand a few minutes and giving it to the patient to drink.

Baldness

One of the most successful remedies ever used is prepared as follows:

| Glycerine 4 ounces | tincture of cantharides 2 drams |
| Tannin 1 dram | oil of capsicum 10 drops |

Apply to the bald spots morning and evening, rub vigorously.

For A Sprain

Take common clay and boil it in white wine vinegar till it is of the thickness of a salve, spread this upon a linen cloth, and apply it to the part affected; let it lie on till it is dry, and if the complaint is not removed apply a second, and it will not fail of a cure.

For the Bite of a Mad Dog—Cat—etc

Immediately wash the wound well with strong salt water and apply over it a blistering plaster. This is proper until a physician can be procured.

When a person's lip or nose is sore with a fever rub it with sweet oil and if that does not remove it, wet it frequently with brandy.

Poisons—Antidote

When it becomes known that a poison has been swallowed, stir salt and ground mustard, of each a heaping tea-spoon, into a glass of water, and have it drank immediately. It is the quickest emetic known.

It should vomit in one minute. Then give the whites of two or three eggs in a cup or two of the strongest coffee. If no coffee, swallow the egg in sweet-cream, and if no cream sweet-milk, if neither, down with the egg.

Tooth Powder

Powdered borax, one-half ounce; powdered chalk, three ounces; add a few drops oil of wintergreen.

A Good Tooth Powder

Precipitated Carbonate of Lime	4 ounces
Pulverized Orris Root	¾ ounce
Pulverized Peruvian Bark	¼ ounce
Pulverized white sugar	¼ ounce

Flavor with that which is most agreeable to the taste   VP

To Make Soap

To 10 gallons of water, add 4 pounds of pearlash and 2 pounds lime, boil it well one hour. Let it settle and add the clear lye to the fat.

Soft Soap

Put on the fire any quantity of lye you choose, and that is strong enough to bear an egg; to each gallon add three quarters of a pound of clean grease, boil it very fast and stir it frequently. A few hours will suffice to make it good soap. When you find by cooling a little on a plate that it is a thick jelly and no grease appears, put in salt in the proportion of one pint to three gallons. Let it boil a few minutes, then pour it in tubs to cool. Should the soap be thin add a little water to that in the plate. Stir it well and by that means ascertain how much water is necessary for the whole quantity; very strong lye will require water to thicken it. Next day cut out the soap, melt it and cool it again. Should cracklings be used, there must be one pound to each gallon. ¾ of your fat will be sufficient.

To Make a Barrel of Soft Soap

Take 12 pounds of potash and dissolve it in as small a quantity of soft water as you well can do it in. Take 6 pounds of clean fat boiling hot and pour into it and stir it well Then pour in a bucket of soft water and stir it right well. Let it stand till next day and then put in another bucket full and so on each day till the barrel is full, stirring it up with each bucket of water.

Excellent Furniture Polish

To be used at least twice a year.

equal parts of		equal parts of
Kerosine		turpentine
olive oil	OR	linseed oil
vinegar		vinegar

Put in bottle and shake thoroughly.

Dampen cloth and add mixture. Then wipe thoroughly dry.

To remove white stains from furniture, rub stains with a thin paste made of olive oil and salt.

Measurements

 10 pounds green peas will serve 25 portions
3½ gallons of punch will serve 100 portions
  1 pound of tea will serve 100 cups
  1 pound of coffee will serve 40 cups
  1 quart cream will serve 35 to 40 people for coffee
20 pounds of old potatoes or 13 pounds of new plus 4 quarts of cream will serve 50 portions of creamed potatoes
  1 quart of strawberries will serve 6 portions when served with ice cream
  6 quarts of ice cream will serve 60 people
13 pounds ham for 50 portions
  1 pound loaf sugar equals 100 cubes
  1 pound butter makes 38 pats

Grammar in Rhyme

1. "Three little words you often see,
Are articles—a, an, and the.
2. A noun's the name of any thing,
As school, or garden, hoop, or swing.
3. Adjectives tell the kind of Noun,
As great, small, pretty, white, or brown.
4. Instead of Nouns the Pronouns stand
Her head, his face, your arm, my hand.
5. Verbs tell of something to be done
To read, count, sing, laugh, jump, or run.
6. How things are done, the adverbs tell,
As slowly, quickly, ill, or well.
7. Conjunctions join the words together
As men and women, wind or weather.
8. The Preposition stands before
A Noun, as in, or through a door.
9. The Interjection shows surprise
As oh! how pretty—ah! how wise.

The whole are called Nine Parts of Speech,
Which reading, writing, speaking, teach.

Whitewash

½ bucket lime salt
1 large double handful cement water to thin

Worm Medicine For Dogs

Syrp. Buckthorn ℨii ℨii
Castor oil ℨiii ℨvi

To Make Perfumes

Take two ounces of red rose buds (the leaves of them must be stripped off), and use only the red part of the flower. Pound them in a mortar, and put to them an ounce of benjamin. When you have pounded them small together, put in three grains of civet, four of ambergris, and twelve of musk; mix these with your fingers, and when you have mixed them well, make them up in little cakes. In the making them up you must put a little flour in the palm of your hand, only to make them hang together; so let them dry in a window.

Fence Post—

To Prevent Rotting

Have a large iron kettle so arranged that you can make and keep the tar hot, then, after having removed the bark, if any, set the end of the post into the tar; and if the tar is not sufficiently deep to take the post into it as far as you wish to tar it, swab it up at least 6 to 10 inches above the ground-line when the post is set; then lift up the post, letting it drip a moment, and lay it away upon rails or poles placed for that purpose, not allowing them to touch each other until dry.

Ants

Sodium Arsenate for Ants. Use one cup sugar in water to make thick syrup then add sodium arsenate, mix well and put in small receptacles where ants are troublesome.

Shoe Blacking

on an economical plan

Oil of vitriol	1 ounce	vinegar	1 quart
Molasses	4 ounces	sweet oil	1 ounce
Ivory black	4 ounces	sour beer	1 pint

It will be very good without the beer.

FOOD FOR THE SICK ROOM

PANADA

Break into a bowl three good sized crackers (arrow root or oat meal are nice) broken into small pieces; pour upon them boiling water and cover close for a minute, then add a tablespoonful of white sugar and a little pure milk. It is an excellent breakfast or supper for a child or an invalid. Instead of the milk the juice of a lemon may be squeezed in and another teaspoonful of sugar added, if there is a fever.

THICKENED MILK

With a little milk, mix smooth a tablespoonful of flour and a pinch of salt. Pour upon it a quart of boiling milk, and when it is thoroughly mixed, put all back into the saucepan and boil up at once, being careful not to burn, and stirring all the time, to keep it perfectly smooth and free from lumps. Serve with slices of dry toast. It is excellent for diarrhoea; this alone will often cure it by scorching the flour before mixing with the milk.

WATER GRUEL

Corn or oat meal two tablespoons, water one quart; boil for ten or fifteen minutes, and add sugar or salt, if desired by the patient.

GROUND RICE GRUEL

Ground rice one heaping tablespoonful, ground cinnamon half a teaspoonful, water one quart; boil slowly for fifteen or twenty minutes, add the cinnamon when it is nearly done boiling, strain and sweeten.

SAGO GRUEL

Sago two tablespoonfuls, water one pint, boil until it thickens, frequently stirring. Wine, sugar and nutmeg may be used if desired.

MILK AND EGGS

Beat up a fresh egg with a grain of salt, pour upon it a pint of boiling milk, stirring it all the time. Serve hot, with or without toast. It is good in case of weakness for an early breakfast, or for a traveller before starting on a journey.

PANNED OYSTERS

Take of butter, a large piece and put into a right hot pan. Liquor of oysters, pour into the pan; so soon as hot, add the oysters, and season light. A few tablespoonfuls of Madeira wine may be added just before taking from the fire.

SOFT CUSTARD

Milk, a pint. Place it to boil; while boiling, take of eggs, three; separate them, and beat up the yolks with sugar enough to sweeten to the taste, and with corn starch, a teaspoonful, rubbed in smoothly. Then pour this egg and corn starch mixture into the pint of boiling milk. Boil for a few minutes, and stir constantly to prevent lumping and burning. When the whole becomes a thick, creamy mass, remove. Have ready, in a dish, some stale sponge-cake, slightly wet with brandy or wine. Pour the custard over it, and cover all with the white of the three eggs whipped stiff, with a half teacupful of pulverized sugar, and flavored with vanilla.

SOFT BOILED EGGS

Fresh eggs for invalids who like them cooked soft, should be put in a pan of boiling water, and set on a part of the stove where they will not boil, for several minutes. At the end of that time they will be like jelly, perfectly soft, but beautifully done and quite digestible by even weak stomachs.

EGG TOAST

Make a soft toast and have ready one or more fresh eggs, which have been boiled twenty minutes; remove the shells, cut them in slices and place upon the toast, with a little butter, pepper and salt; without the butter they may be eaten with impunity by the most delicate invalid, as an egg cooked for twenty minutes is really more easy of digestion than one that is termed "boiled soft."

MILK TOAST

This is a favorite dish with nearly all sick people, when they are getting well. Cut stale bread in rather thin slices, toast a fine brown and lay them in a deep dish. Meanwhile boil a quart of new milk in a lined sauce pan in which you have first put a very little cold water to prevent burning. As soon as it boils pour it over the toast, cover and serve quick. For an invalid no butter should be put in the milk. Some people put in a thickening of flour, but this spoils it for many.

SOFT TOAST

Some invalids like this very much indeed, and nearly all do when it is nicely made.

Toast well, but not too brown, a couple of thin slices of bread; put them on a warm plate and pour over boiling water; cover quickly with another plate of the same size and drain the water off; remove the upper plate, butter the toast, put it in the oven one minute and then cover again with a hot plate and serve at once.

BEEF TEA

Cut up a pound of rump steak into small pieces, and put it into a jar putting a very small quantity of luke warm water into the jar with it, cork tightly and put the jar into a kettle of warm water; the water should be allowed to boil for a considerable time; the jar should then be removed and the juice drained off. The tea may be salted a little and a teaspoonful given at a time.

MUTTON TEA

Take one pound of mutton, remove the fat and cut the meat in small pieces; pour half a pint of boiling water over it, and let it stand near a fire for half an hour, and then boil for one hour, strain through a sieve or cloth, add salt to suit the taste. A very nourishing diet.

CHICKEN TEA

Take off the skin and all the fat of the fowl, and boil the fowl till very tender, with just sufficient water to cover it, and add a little salt. Take the chicken out of the liquor when boiled, and let the liquor remain till cold to let all the fat rise to the surface, which should then be skimmed off. The tea should be heated when given to the patient. It is a very delicate, nourishing food, and will set well on the stomach when so weak as to be able to retain but little food.

ANOTHER BEEF TEA

The latest and most approved method of making beef tea, is to take a half pound of good steak, broil slightly over hot coals; then lay into a shallow dish, and with a sharp knife, gash it on both sides until it is cut into mere shreds; then pour a half pint of boiling water over it, and scrape hard for a few moments, when all the nutriment of the beef will be extracted. This is the easiest, quickest, and by many thought to be the best method.

TOAST WATER

Toast slightly a piece of bread and add to it boiling water; it may be sweetened, if preferred, and flavored with a little lemon or orange peel.

LEMONADE

This is invaluable in fevers and also in rheumatic affections. Rub the lemons soft, cut them half through the center and squeeze out the juice. Take out the seeds with a teaspoon. Put two tablespoons of white sugar to each lemon, and fill up with cold or boiling water according as you desire the lemonade hot or cold. Two medium sized lemons will make a pint or more.

ROAST APPLES

These can nearly always be eaten with safety, when they are eaten with relish. Choose good sized, fair apples of a tart and juicy, but not a sour kind. Rub them off clean, and put them in a rather slow oven, which may increase in warmth, so that they shall be thoroughly done in an hour. When so soft that the savory pulp breaks through the browned skin in every direction, take them out, sift white sugar over them, and carry one at a time on a saucer to the patient.

ANCIENT COOKERY

The MS. from whence the following pages are transcribed, is without title or date, or the name of the author. It is bound up with some other treatises upon Regimen and Medicine; one of which is stiled: "De Regimine Sanitatis; edita a Magistro Johanne de Tholeto. AD 1285." And it is evident from the hand, that these treatises were written soon after that time; that is, early in the 15th Century; but they were probably then transcribed from originals, which had been long before composed by persons of fame and celebrity in the practise of Regimen and Cookery.

Cabaches

Take cabaches and cut hom on foure, and mynce onyons there with, and the white of lekes, and cut hom smal, and do all togedur in a potte, and put thereto gode broth, and let hit boyle; and colour hit with saffron, and put thereto pouder douce, and serve hit forthe.

Rys in Potage of Flesh

Take rys and wash hom clene, and put hom in pot, and do thereto gode brothe, and let hit seethe tyl the rys bee ynough, then do thereto almonde mylke, and colour hit wyth saffron, and let hit boyle, and serve hit forthe.

Grene Pesen Wyth Bakon

Take old pesen, and boyle hom in gode flesh broth that bacon is sothen in, then take hom and bray hom in a morter, and temper hom wyth the broth, and strayne hom thurgh a streynour, and do hom in the pot, ande let hom boyle tyl thai alye homself, and serve hit forthe wyth Bacon.

Chekyns in Sauge

Take chekenes and make hom cleve and choppe hom, but a hole one for a lorde, and sethe hem, and when thai byn sothen pul of the skyn; then take sauge and parsel and grinde hom smal, and do therto harde zolkes of eggus ynowe, and tempur hom up with wyn, and drawe hom up thurgh a streynour into the pot; then loke hit be thik, and do therto clowes and sugur, and pouder of canel, and in the settynge doun put thereto a lytel vynegur; then couche the chekyns in platers and poure the sewe theron, and serve hit forthe colde.

Stewet Beef to Potage

Take faire ribbes of beeff, or elles take other gode beef, and smyte hit on peces, and wash hit clene and do hit in a pot, and put thereto a lytel watur, and a gode dele wyne; and take onyons ynogh, and mynce hom, and do thereto, and gode herbes, cut hom small and put thereto; and take bred stepet in brothe, and draw hit thurgh a streynour, and do hit thereto, and coverr hit wel, and let hit wel sethe; and do therto pouder of cloves and maces, and colour hit with saffron; and in the settynge down do thereto a lytel vynegur medelet wyth pouder of canel, and serve hit forthe, and do thereo raisynges of Corance.

A Drye Stewe For Beeff

Take a grete flaffe, and do thi bee therin, and do therto onyons myced, and hole clowes, and maces, and raisinges of Corance, and wyn; then stop hit welle, and sethe it in a pot with watur, or in a cawdron, but take gode care that no watur goe in; or take a faire urthen pot, and lay hit well with splentes in the bothum, that the flessh neigh hit not; then take rybbes of beef or faire leches, and couche hom above the splentes, and do thereto onyons mynced, and clowes, and maces, and pouder of pepur and wyn, and stop hit well that no eyre goo oute, and sethe hit wyth esy fyre.

Sause for a Goose

Take a faire panne, and set hit under the goose whill sche rostes, and kepe clene the grese that droppes thereof, and put therto a godele of wyn and a litel vynegur, and verjus, and onyons mynced or garlek; then take the gottes of the goose, and slitte hom, and scrape hom clene in watur and salt, and so wassh hom, and sethe hom, and hak hom smal; then do all this togedur in a postenet, and do therto raisinges of Corrance, and pouder of pepur, and of gynger, and of canell, and hole clowes, and maces, and let hit boyle, and serve hit forthe.

Hares in Padell

Take Hares and slee hom, and pyke hom clene, and hewe hom on gobettes, and put hom in a pot wyth the blode, and feth hom, and when thai byn ynogh, take hom up and do hom in colde watur, and clense the broth into a faire pot and do other gode broth thereto; and take almondes, and bray hom, and tempur hit wyth the same broth, and put hit thereto, and onyons parboyled and mynced, and do hit in the pot, and set hit on the fyre, and let hit boyle, and do thereto powder of clowes, and of canell and maces, and lytel vynegar; then take the flesh wele washen, and the bones clene pyked out and do hom in the pot to the broth, and let hit boyle, and serve hit forth.

Bore in Egurdouce

Take fressh braune and sethe hit, and kerve hit in thynne leches, and lay three in a dysshe, then take date and raisynges of Corance, and wassh hom clene, and bray hom in a mortar, and in the braying cast therto a few clows, and draw hom up with clarre or other swete wyne, and do hit in a pot, and let hit boyle, and do thereto a gode dele of sugur or honey, and ginger mynced, and in the settynge doun, put therto pouder of canel and vynegur medelet togedur, and colour hit with saunders and saffron depe; then take pynes or almondes blaunched and drye hom in faire grees, and then take hom up and let hom drie, and when thow wilt dresse up thi braune do the pynes in the pot and poure the syrip thereon, and serve hit forthe.

Alaunder of Moton

Take moton of the legge, and seth hit tendur by hitself, and qwhen it is sothen take and braie hit in a morter, or hewe hit smal with a knyfe, and putte hit in a pot and boile hit with the same broth; and take saffrone, and pouder of clowes, and of canel, and put therto, and sethe hit, and serve hit forthe.

Gele of Flesshe

Take veel or pyggus, or capons, or hennus, or gryse, and sethe hom wel togedur a longe tyme in watur and wyn; then take oute the fleshe and clense the brothe, and a blowe of the grees, and put therin thi pouder, and colour hit with turnefole, or with ynde, or with alkenet, or saunders, or saffron; and do therto sugur or honey, and let hit boyle; and if thou wyl make hit white, take er thow clefe thi brothe, and tempur hit with almondes mylk, and then clense hit, and do thy pouder therto, and sethe it, and if hit be on fyssh day, make hit on the same manere of playsse or of codlynge, or of eles, or of pykes, or of soles, or tenches. And if thow wil make hit of two maner of colours in a dysshe, take and make a rounde of paste, and lay hit in the mydwarde of the chargeoure, and poure in the gele, and when hit is colde, take oute the paste, and poure the other of another colour, and serve hit forthe colde.

Malardes in Cyne

Take malardes, and make hom cleve, and chop hom, and sethe hom with gode brothe of beef in a pot, and do therto onyons mynced grete, and do therto wyne and pouder of pepur; then take bredde, and stepe hit in brothe, and draw hit up, and do hit in a pot, and clowes, and maces, and pynes, and colour hit with saunders and saffron; and put therto sugur or honey, and in the settynge doun do therto a lytel vynegur, and serve hit forthe.

Payn Ragun

Take clarified honey, and sugur cypre, and boyle hom togedur with esy fyre, that hit brenne not, and when hit hase boylet awhile take up a drope, and do hit in a lytel watur, and loke if it honge togedur; then take hit from the fyre, and do thereto a gret quantitie of pynes, and pouder of ginger, and stere hit well togeder, tyl hit begynne to thik; then take and cast hit on a wete table, and leche hit, and serve hit forthe with roste on flessh day, or fried mete on fyssh day.

At a Feeste Roiall

PECOKKES SHALL BE DIGHT ON THIS MANERE

Take and flee off the skynne with the fedurs tayle and the nekke, and the hed theon; then take the skyn with all the fedurs, and lay hit on a table abrode; and strawe theron grounden comyn; then take the pecokke, and roste hym, and endore hym with rawe zolkes of egges; and when he is rosted take hym of, and let hym coole awhile, and take and sowe hym in his skyn, and silde his combe, and so serve hym forthe with the last cours.

Pevrate Sause for Veel or Venison

Take bred and frie it in greese, and draw hit up with the brothe and vynegur and do thereto pouder of pepur, and of clowes, and let hit boyle and serve hit forthe.

Syrip for a Capon or Faysant

Take almondes, and bray hom, and tempur hom up with wyn, and make a gode thik mylke, and colour hit with saffron, and do hit in a postenet, and put therto gode plentie of pynes, and raisynges of corance, and do therto pouder of gynger, and of clowes, and of galyngale, and of canel, and let hit boyle, and put sugar therto; and when the capons, or the faisantes byn rosted, take and poure the syrip above, and serve hit forthe.

To Kepe a Salt Laumpray Al Yere for Apairinge

Take a laumpray, and stop hym with salt wel, and take a gode thik canevas, and take thik lies of wyne, and lay theron; and then take the laumpray, and hille hym in the lies, and rolle then the canevas togeder, and lay hit in a place where non arie entres but lytel, and so thow schalt save hym gode throughoute the zere.

Appelun for a Lorde, in Opyntide

Take appuls cut of tweyne or of foure, and sethe hom, and bray hom in a morter, and then streyne hom; and when thai byn Streyned, do hom in a pot, and let hom sethe tyl the joust and water be sothen oute, and put then therto a lytel vernage, or other swete wyne, and cast therto sugre, and when hit is sothen in the settynge doune of the pot, put therto a few zolkes of eyren beten and streyned, and set up the potage, Stondyng, and put therto a lytel water of euerose, and stere hit wel togeder, and dresse hit up stondynge on leches in disshes, and straw aboven blomes of qwerdelynges or of other gode frute; and serve hit forthe.

This potage is in sesonne April, May and June, while the trees blowen. This potage may be made in Lenten, and also in Opentyde, on this same manere, withouten eyren.

Gele of Fysshe

Take tenches, pykes, eles, turbot and plays, or other gode fyssh, and cut hom on peces, and scalde hom, and wash hom clene, and drie hom in a panne, and do therto wyn a godele, and the thridde parte vynegur, and a lytel watur, and sethe hit well; when hit is innowe take hit up, and pyke out the bones clene, and put hit in a faire vessel; then cole thi brothe thurgh a clene clothe into a faire vessell; and caste therto gode pouder, and colour hit with saffron ynogh, and set hit on the fire, and sethe hit wel, and scome hit clene; when hit is sothen do of the grese clene, and poure above the fisshe, and serve hit forthe colde.

To Make a Salt Laumpray Fresshe

For to make a salt laumpray fresshe in one night, or elles in foure, or fyve houres; take the laumpray, and wassh hym twyse or thries wel in lewe water, and then take ale dristes, and lies, and lewe water medeled togeder; and let hym stepe therin one night or lesse, and then wassh hym oute with lew water, and sethe hym, and he schal be fresshe ynogh at a say.

Medicina Optima

ET EXPERTA PRO STOMACHO ET PRO CAPITE IN ANTIQUO HOMINEM

Take ginger, cane, long pepur, rose-marine, graynes, of ichone a quartrone; then take clowes, maces, spikenarde, nut-mukes, gardamour, galingal, of ichone one unce; liqui aloes, calamy, aromatici, croci, rubarbi, reupontici of ichone nine pennyweight; make of all this a gros pouder; then take a galone of swete wyne, oseye, or bastard, and cast therto, and do hit in a clene pot of urthe, and let hit stonde al a nyght togeder, and stir hit oft, and melle hit well, and let hit stonde tyl on the morwen, tyl hit be clere; then take out the clere from the pouder, and put hit into a glasse; then have a bagge redy of faire lynnyn clothe, that hit be made brode above, and scharpe benethe. And therin put the pouder, and honge the bagge tytwene two tressels, and let hit renne oute qwat hit wil; and then take alle that rennes oute from the pouder, and that clere that thow hadst before of the wyne, and medel therwith two pounde of lofe sugre or more, tyl hit be right swete; and therof cast aboven the bagge, and let hit renne thorugh esiliche tyl that hit be ronnen al thorugh; and that is clepet clarry. And therof take yche day, fyve spoonfull in the morwen, with three soppes of bred wel soked therin, and forbere hedes of fysshe and of flesshe; and also forbere goutous metes, and unholsome.

Frissure

Take hares hilt, and wasshe hom in brothe of beef with alle the blode, and boyle the blode, and skym hit wel, and then parboyle the hares, and chope hom, and frie hom in faire grees, and caste hom into a pot, and let hom boyle ensemble; and put therto onyons mynced, clowes, maces, pynes, and reisynges of corance, and draw up chippes of bred with wyne, and put therto; and also pouder of pepur, ande of canel, and sugre, and colour hit with saffron: ande in the settyinge doun alay hit with a lytel vynegur, and serve hit forthe.

Toste to Potage

Take wyn and honey, and bete hit well togedur, and sethe hit welle, and scome hit welle, and put therto pouder of pepur, and of gynger; and take and toste bredde, and dresse hit forthe, and poure and sewe above.

Soppes in Fenell

Take the blades of fenell, and cutte hom, but not too smalle, and sethe hom in watur, ande oyle, and mynce onyons and do therto, and colour hit with saffron, and do therto pouder, and take and toste bredde, and dresse hit forthe, and poure the sewe above.

Caudel Rennyng

Take vernage, or other gode wyne, and zolkes of eyren beten, and streyned, and put therto suger, and colour hit with saffron, and sethe hit tyl hit begyn to boyle, and strawe pouder of ginger theron; and serve hit forthe.

Slitte Soppes

Take the white of lekes, and slytte hom, and sethe hom in wyn, and oyl, and do therto pouder and toste bredde, and do as to foresaide.

Tart for Lenton

Take figges and raisinges, and wassh hom in wyne, and grinde hom, and appuls and peres clene pared, and corke tane out; then take fresh samon, or codlynge, or hadok, and grinde hit, and medel hit all togedur, and do hit in a coffyn, and do therto pouder of ginger, and of canelle, and clowes, and maces; and plaunte hit above with pynes, or almondes, and prunes, and dates quartert, then cover thi coffyn, and bake hit and serve hit forthe.

Crem of Almonde Mylk

Take almonde mylk, and boyle hit, and when hit is boylet take hit from the fyre, and springe theron a lytel vynegur; then take and cast hit on a clothe, and cast theron sugur, and when hit is colde gedur hit together, and leche hit in dysshes, and serve hit forthe.

Caboches

Take caboches, and washe hom in clene water, and boyle hom wel, and at the seconde boyle, take hom doun off the fyre, and presse hom wel tyl the water be clene oute, and then cutte hom in grete peces, and caste hom in the broth of beef, and seth hom up with maribones, and colour hom then with saffrone, and thikke hit with grated bred; but for a lorde hit schal be thikked with yolkes of eyren beten, and thenne let hit ones boyle, and serve hit forthe.

Jussel of Flessh

Take brothe of capons boyled with gode herbes, with parsel and sauge, and other gode herbes, and colour hit with saffron; ande for a lorde, take clene zolkes of eyren beten, and cast into the brothe, and let hit boyle, and stere hit wel tyl hit crudde togeder, and then dresse hit in disshes, and serve hit. But for Commons, take eyren zolkes and al beten, and medelet with grated bred, and sethe it up as thou diddest before; and serve hit forthe.

Crem Boyled

Take crem of cowe mylke, and zolkes of egges, and bete hom wel togedur, and do hit in a pot, and let hit boyle tyl hit be stondynge, and do therto sugur, and colour hit with saffron and dresse hit forthe in leches, and plante therin floures of borage or vyolet.

Turtelettys of Fruture

Take fygges, and grind hom small, and do therto pouder of clowes, and of pepur, and sugur, and saffron, and close hom in foyles of dogh, and friet hom, and flawme hom with honey, and serve hit forthe.

Spices and Herbs

Members of the cabbage family may be flavored with a pinch of nutmeg.

Green beans may be seasoned with Summer Savory.

Chicken and Pork may be seasoned with Sweet Marjoram.

JR

Omelettes and fine herbs. A good combination is: A pinch each of basil, summer savory, thyme, chives OR Basil, thyme, parsley, sweet marjoram OR Chives, parsley, savory, basil. CPR

MEMORANDA

MEMORANDA

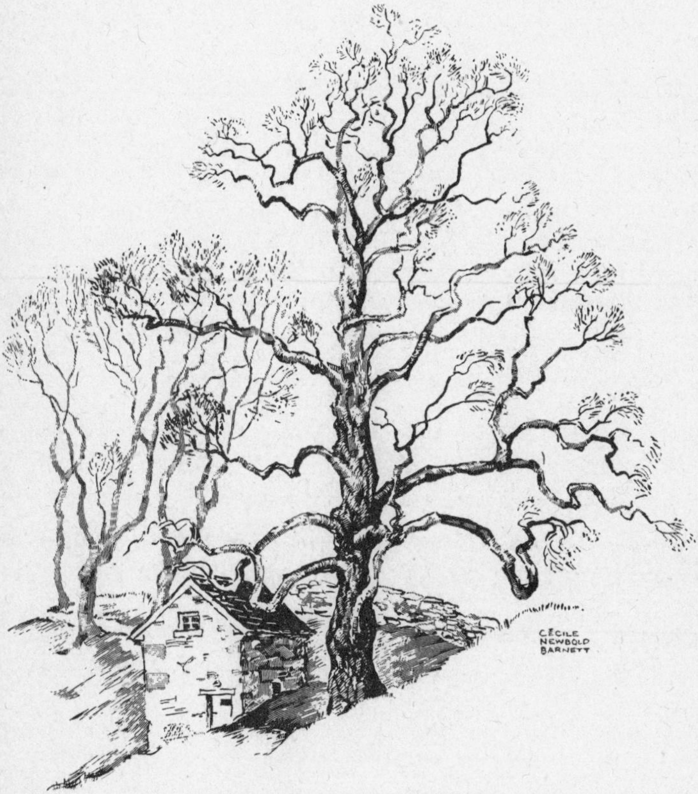
CÉCILE
NEWBOLD
BARNETT

CONTRIBUTORS

Mrs T E B.................................Mrs T E Biddle
    C E B.................................Dr Cathryn E Bishop
Mrs H B...................................Mrs Harry Brackbill
Mrs M B...................................Mrs Milton Brackbill
    M D B.................................Mrs Ellis Y Brown Jr
    C U B.................................Mrs Henry Ball Baker

    M H C.................................Mrs W Poyntell Canby
    M C......................................Mrs Willoughby Chesley
    M C......................................Mrs George M Coates
Mrs R C...................................Mrs Roger Combs
    I P C..................................Miss Isabel Chase
    E A C..................................Miss Edith A Cray
Mrs P C...................................Mrs Philip Chase

    J D......................................Miss Josephine Doran

    M C E..................................Mildred C Edge
Mrs E.......................................Mrs Eshleman

    C G......................................Mrs Arthur R Guy
    E G......................................Miss Ellen Gooding

    F H......................................Aunt Fanny Haldeman
    R B H..................................Mrs Butler N Heilner
    E H......................................Mrs E L Hanson
    A T H..................................Mrs Lardner Howell

    J J.......................................Miss Jane Jacobs

Mrs R K...................................Mrs Rose King

Mrs A L...................................Mrs August Lohnhoff
Mrs S G L...............................Mrs S G Lineinger
Mrs L.......................................Mrs Longaker

F M..Miss Frances McIlvain
E P M..Miss Edith P Moore
C M..Miss Claire Muldowney
M H M..Margaret Howell Maull
M M..Mrs Thomas McCutcheon
E T M..Elizabeth T McIlvaine
M M..Mrs Charles Mead
L B M..Mrs W E Mullestein

M O..Dr Maurice Ostheimer

V P..Mrs Charles Penrose
Z P..Mrs Charles Perrin

C P R..Mrs Adolph G Rosengarten
F R..Frederick Roye
J R..Miss Joyce Reisener

M S..Mrs Charles W Shreiner

Mrs H S T......................................Mrs Howard S Taylor
K T..Mrs Horace Thomas
L T..Mrs Richard Thomas
E M T..Mrs Frank M Taylor
E B T..Mrs George H Taylor Jr
S T..Miss Sarah Thomas
E N T..Mrs John Thomas

R W W..Robert W Wolcott
K M W..Mrs R M Woods

B F Y..Mrs Wilson S Yerger
F B Y..Mrs Charles Young
Mrs Y..Mrs L F Yocum

INDEX

A

Almond Pudding, 166
Alaunder of Moton, 239
Ancient Cookery, 236
Angel Food Waldorf, 157
Angel Food or Snow Flake Cake, 148
Ants, 231
Appelun for a Lorde, in Opyntide, 242
Appetizers, 15-16
Apples, 108
Apple Batter Pudding, 173
Apple Chutney, 210
Apple Dessert, Crunchy, 179
Apples, Casserole of, 185
Apple Dowdy (100 years old), 177
Apple Rings, 35
Apple Sauce, 183
Apple Sauce Cake, 143
Apple Torte, 174
Artichokes, French, 106
At a Feeste Roiall, 241

Biscuits, Short Bread, 132
Biscuits—Sour Milk (100 years old), 132
Bite of a Mad Dog—Cat, etc., 228
Blackberry Jam, 213
Black Cake, 182
Blanc Mange, 175
Blueberry Cake, 140
Boiled Dutch Dressing, 120
Boiled Loaf, 170
Bore in Egurdonce, 239
Bouquet Garni, 23, 203
Breads, 127-133
Brine Pickles That Will Remain Hard, 206
Brown Sugar Cake, 147
Bread Mixture, 127
Broccoli Salad, 115
Brown Bread, 128
Buns, 131
Buns, Potato, 131
Buns, Quick Cinnamon, 131
Butter, 215
Butter, Herb, 15
Butter, Lemon, 216

B

Bacon, To Make, 223
Baking Powder—To Make, 221
Baldness, 227
Barley Soup, 24
Beans—Ragou of French, 107
Beans, Salting of, 205
Beef and Pork, To Cure, 58
Beef Collops, 58
Beef Steaks in Ale, 59
Beef Steaks in Wine, 59
Beef Stew with Savory Dumplings, 52
Beef Stroganoff, 58
Beef, To Stuff a Round of, 50
Beef Tea, 235
Berries, 204
Beverages, 191-195

C

Cabaches, 237
Caboches, 245
Cabbage, 104
Cabbage, Real German Red, 105
Cabbage, Red, 104, 105
Cabbage with Rosemary, 105
Cabbage, Stuffed, 49
Cakes, 139-159
Calves Feet Jelly, 212
Calves Head—Turtle Fashion, 57
Cancer, For a, 227
Candied Orange or Grapefruit Peel, 210
Canning, 204
Caramels, Hard, 225
Caramels, Soft, 225

Caramels, Sugar, 226
Carrot Souffle, 104
Carrots with Sweet Marjoram, 104
Castor Oil—How to give Children, 226
Caudel Rennyng, 244
Cauliflowers, A Raggoo of, 107
Caviar, Red, 15
Cedar Syrup, 212
Cheese, 93
Cheese Biscuits, Snappy, 15
Cheese, Cream—to Make, 94
Cheese Herbs, 92
Cheese Cake Pie, 156
Cheese Pigs for Snacks, 94
Cheese Spread, 92
Chekyns in Sauge, 237
Cherries, 204
Chicken, 80
Chicken Salad, Californian, 119
Chicken Croquettes, 81
Chicken Curry, 82
Chicken Tea, 235
Chili Sauce—100 years old, 201
Chocolate Cakes 1872, 179
Chocolate Roll, 165
Chocolate Spice Cakes, 141
Cholera Marbus, 227
Chowder, Clam, 25
Chowder, Fish, 24
Christmas Bread, 129
Chutney Sauce—Mrs. Brown's, 207
Cider Vinegar, 214
Cinnamon Flop, 179
Cinnamon Fluff, 171
Cinnamon Sauce for Waffles (hot), 70
Claret Cup, 194
Cocoanut Cream Candy, 224
Cocktail Schaw, 195
Cod, Boiled Salt—The Italian Way, 35
Cod Sounds, 36
Codfish Balls, Cherry, 16
Coffee Cake, Baking Powder, 149
Cole Slaw, 118
Cole Slaw Dressing, 118
Company Dessert, 170
Convent Pie, 50
Cookies, 153

Cookies, Brown Sugar, 149
Cookies, Chocolate (Aunt Ruth's), 151
Cookies, Christmas Crisps, 153
Cookies, Date, 173
Cookies, Fancy Sugar, 150
Cookies, Fudge, 153
Cookies, Ginger, 150
Cookies, Graham Crackers, 149
Cookies, Josephine's Oatmeal, 152
Cookies, Molasses, 150
Cookies, Oatmeal, 151
Cookies, Peanut Butter, 151
Cookies, Pecan, 152
Cookies, Spekulatins, A good Crisp Spice, 152
Cookies, Swedish Orange, 152
Corn, 101
Corn and Beans—Creamed, 101
Corn Fritters, 101
Corn Oysters, 102
Corn Pudding, 102
Corn Souffle, 100
Corn Bread, Steamed, 128
Cough—For a, 226
Cough—To Cure a, 227
Crab Meat, 37
Crab—Tomato Soup, 18
Cranberry Jelly, 208
Cream Sauce, 72
Creme Brulee, 185
Cream Cake, 142
Crem of Almonde Mylk, 245
Crem Boyled, 245
Crullers, 130
Cucumber Aspic, 120
Cucumber Relish, 210
Cucumbers—Stewed, 103
Cumberland Sauce, 72
Cup—Eggless Cake, 145
Currant Jelly, 213

D

Date and Nut Bread, 157
Dessert Wine Jelly, 167
Desserts, 165-186
Dinner Dish, 49
Disordered Stomach, 226

[254]

Dried Fruits and Vegetables, 203
Drye Stewe For Beeff, A, 238
Duck, Casserole with Sour Cream, 83
Duck—Wild, 80
Dumpling Batter, 52
Dumplings for Soup, 26
Dumplings Fried in Caramel Syrup, 165

E

Eggs, 222
Eggs and Cheese, 89-94
Eggs Casserole—Stuffed, 90
Eggs Humpty-Dumpty, 91
Egg-Nog, 193
Egg Plant—Turkish, 105
Eggs—Poached with Cucumbers, 91
Eggs—Scotch, 92
Eggs, Shirred on Tomatoes, 91
Eggs, Stuffed, 92
Egg Toast, 234
Emergency Soups (Canned), 23
Entrees and Meat, 43-63

F

Feather Cake, 140
Fence Post, 231
Fish, 33-37
Fish Chowder, 24
Fish and Spinach Casserole, 51
Foamy Sauce, 69
Foie Gras Maison Potter, 16
Frissure, 243
Floating Island, 178, 181
Force Meat, 48
Frosting, Chocolate Velvet, 159
Fruit Salad or Dessert, 116
Fruit Salad, Mother's, 117
Fruits to Keep, 221
Fudge, 225
Furniture Polish, 229

G

Game and Fowl, 79-83
Gele of Flesshe, 240

Gele of Fysshe, 242
Ginger Bread, 154
Gingerbread, 182
Gingerbread Cake, 144
Gingerbread, Soft—or Spiced, 144
Gingerbread, Soft, 154, 155
Ginger Snaps, 153
Gnocchi Parisien, 45
Goose—Roasted, 81
Gooseberry Sauce for Mackerel, 71
Grammar in Rhyme, 230
Grape Butter, 207
Grape Catsup, 208
Grape Jam—Mrs. Ryan's, 215
Grape Jelly, 206
Grape Juice, 191
Grene Pesen Wyth Bakon, 237
Greens, 118
Green Tomato Mince Meat, 205

H

Haddock, 33
Ham, 55, 223
Ham, How to Bake a, 56
Hams, To Cure, 56
Ham Loaf, 47
Ham, To Make a, 215
Ham Mousse, 56
Hamburgers, 62
Hares in Padell, 239
Hawaiian Jam, 208
Heavenly Salad, 115
Herb Butter, 15
Herbs, 202
Holiday Cocktail, 193
Hollandaise Sauce, 73
Honey Boy, 170

I

Ice Cream, Chocolate, 180
Ice Cream, Peach, 181
Ice Cream Snow Balls, 172
Ice Cream, Strawberry, 181
Ice Cream, Vanilla, 181
Iced-Tea Kentucky Mint Syrup, 192
Indian Muffins, 184

[255]

J

Jackson Jumbles, 158
Japonica Jelly, 209
Jellied Vegetable Salad, 116
Jug Yeast, 224
Jumbles, 182
Jussel of Flessh, 245

K

Kepe a Salt Laumpray Al Yere for Apairinge, To, 241

L

Lady Cake, 140, 144
La Maise Sauce, 71
Lamb Curry with Rice, 54
Lamb Stew, 48
Lavender Compound, 213
Layer Cake, 142
Lemon Cake, 139
Lemonade, 236
Lemon Sauce, 72
Lettuce with Sour Cream Dressing, 119
Liver Loaf, 45
Loaf Cake, 143
Loaf Spice Cake, 145
Lobster a la Newburg, 34

M

Macaroons, 156
Macaroons, Cherry, 156
Make a Salt Laumpray Fresshe, To, 242
Malardes in Cyne, 240
May Wine, 191
Measurements, 230
Meat Balls in Tomato Sauce, 50
Meat Loaf, 53
Meat Loaf a la Boop, 53
Meat Loaf, Stuffed, 54
Medicina Optima, 243
Meringues, Sherry, 158
Milk and Eggs, 233

Milk Toast, 234
Mint Julep, 195
Miscellaneous, 221-246
Mother's Fruit Salad, 117
Muffins, 130
Muffins, Corn Meal, 130
Mulligatawny Soup, 22
Mushrooms—Baked, 102
Mushrooms, Creamed, 103
Mushroom Soup, Cream of, 23
Mutton Tea, 235
Mutton, Venison Fashion, 57

N

Nectar Dressing for Fruit Salad, 121
Nectar Dressing, II, 121
Newburg Sauce, 34
Newbury Sauce, 69
Noodles, Reading, 43
Nut Bread—Black Walnut, 176
Nut Cake, 148
Nut Wafers, 154

O

Okra Soup, 24
One Gallon Pitcher, 194
Onion Pie, 44
Onion Sauce Plain, 70
Onion Soup, 21
Onions, Glazed, 109
Orange Bread, 128
Orange Cake, 145
Oyster Sauce, 69
Oysters Supreme, 33

P

Panada, 232
Panned Oysters, 233
Partridge, 82
Parsley, 206
Payn Ragun, 240
Peaches, 204
Peach Marmalade, 207
Peach Melba, 184

Peach and Orange Marmalade, 206, 207
Peanut Butter Soup, 24
Pears, 204
Pears, Baked, 182
Pear-Lime Salad, 120
Pear Marmalade, 209
Pears Sublime, 183
Pecans—Toasted, 184
Pepper Hash, 213
Pepper Relish, 209
Peppermint Drops, 225
Perfumes, To Make, 231
Pevrate Sause for Veel or Venison, 241
Philadelphia Pepper Pot, 22
Pickle for Beef or Pork (Knickerbocker), 211
Pickled Oysters, 211
Pickled Plums or Cherries, 214
Pickled Tomatoes, 212
Pie, Apple Cream, 176
Pie, Boston Cream, 165
Pie, Lemon, 179
Pie, Lemon Sponge, 167
Pie, Nesselrode, 177
Pie, Peach Sour Cream, 176
Pie, Pumpkin, 183
Pie, Raisin, 168
Pie, Shoo Fly, 167
Pie, Shoo Fly—Mrs. Brackbill's, 174
Pie, Shoo Fly (Dutch Way), 175
Pie, Strawberry, 174
Pigeons, 83
Pigs in Blankets, 46
Pineapple Punch, 192
Planters Punch, 194
Plums, 204
Plum Cake, 140
Poisons—Antidote, 228
Poke Weed with Pennsylvania Dutch Dressing, 108
Popovers, 130
Pork Cake, 44
Pork Pie, Cheshire, 60
Potage Germiny, 27
Potatoes—Boiled, 100
Potatoes—Creamed, 100
Pot Roast, Swedish, 59
Pound or Queen, 144

Preserves, 201-215
Preserved Apples, 209
Prune Salad Mold, 117
Puff Cake, 146
Pudding, Apple, 182
Pudding, Bag, 178
Pudding, Bread, 167
Pudding, Bread, Aunt Grace's, 178
Pudding, Buttermilk, 174
Pudding, Chocolate, Baked, 184
Pudding, Chocolate Ice Box, 185
Pudding, Cream, 168
Pudding, Danish Lemon, 167
Pudding, Indian Baked (100 years old), 177
Pudding, Plain, A Fine, 168
Pudding, Plum, Christmas, 180
Pudding, Potato, 181
Pudding, Rice, 183
Pudding, Rice, for Baking, 169
Pudding, Rice—Superb, 169
Pudding, Sweet Potato, 186

Q

Quail, 82
Queen or Pound Cake, 144
Queen Cakes, 146
Quince Marmalade, 213

R

Rabbit, An English, 90
Rabbit, A Scotch, 90
Rabbit, A Welsh, 89
Rabbit—Fricasseed, 79
Raggoo of Lamb, A, 57
Ragout of Livers, 63
Raisin Cake, Boiled, 141
Raisin Sauce, 55
Raisin Sauce for Ham, 70
Raisin Sunflower Salad, 117
Refrigerator Cheese Cake, 147
Rice Bread, 129
Rice Gruel, Ground, 233
Rhubarb Crunch, 172
Roast Apples, 236
Rosemary, 222
Rys in Potage of Flesh, 237

Rusk—Bread, 133
Russian Dressing, 73

S

Salad, 118
Salad Dressing for Two, 71
Sago Gruel, 233
Salads, 115-121
Salmon Puffles, 35
Sandwiches, 224
Sauce Robert, 71
Sauce for Venison, 69
Sauces, 69-73
Saus, 49
Sause for a Goose, 238
Sausage, 61
Sausage, Bologna, 61
Sausage, Virginia, 51
Scotch Cakes, 148
Scrapple, 61
Shad Roe, 36
Shoe Blacking, 232
Shrimp Creole, 37
Sick Room Food, 232
Slitte Soppes, 244
Smelts, To Fry, 37
Snow Flake or Angel Food Cake, 148
Soap—To Make, 228
Soap, Soft, 229
Soap, Soft, To Make a Barrel, 229
Soft Boiled Eggs, 234
Soft Custard, 233
Soft Toast, 234
Sole, 33
Sole Marguery, 34
Soppes in Fenell, 244
Sorrel, 26
Souffle a la Refrigerator, 46
Soups, 21-27
Southern Salad, 121
Southern Spoon Bread, 127
Spaghetti—Italian, 48
Spaghetti Sauce (Mexico City), 47
Spaghetti S S "France" 1930, 47
Spareribs, Sweet and Sour, 55
Spices and Herbs, 246
Spiced Peaches, 202, 206

Spiced Seckle Pears, 206
Spiced Watermelon, 201
Spinach, 106
Spinach Ring with Mushrooms, 106
Spiritual Facts, 194
Sponge Cake, 148, 159
Sponge Cake, Hot Milk, 171
Sprain, For a, 227
Squabs, Roasted, 83
Stewet Beef to Potage, 238
Strawberries, 205
Strawberry Delight, 183
Strawberry Shortcake, 149
Sugar Nut Candy, 226
Sunshine Cake, 146
Sugared Pop Corn, 225
Supreme Salad, 119
Sweetbreads, To Fry, 60
Sweet Potatoes—Baked Mashed, 99
Sweet Potato Pie, 99
Syllabubs, 192
Syllabubs Everlasting, 193
Syllabubs Whip, 194
Syrip for a Capon or Faysant, 241

T

Tarts, 155
Tarts, German Sand, 155
Tartar Sauce, 72
Tart for Lenton, 244
Tea Biscuits, Irish, 158
Tea Biscuits, New York, 158
Tea Cake (to be eaten while warm), 143
Thickened Milk, 232
Toast Water, 236
Tomatoes, 204
Tomato Catsup—Wilson Rule-1884, 207
Tomato-Crab Soup, 26
Tomatoes, Fried, 108
Tomato Ketchup, 211
Tomato Mustard, 215
Tooth Powder, 228
Toste to Potage, 244
Trifle, 171
Turkey Hash, White Sauce for, 83
Turtelettys of Fruture, 246

V

Veal, 62
Veal Cutlet, 62
Vegetables, 99-109
Vichysoisse, 23

W

Waffles, 131, 132
Warner's Gout Cordial, 208

Water Gruel, 232
Welsh Rarebit, 89
White Fricassee, 80
White Nut Cake, 142
Whitewash, 231
Wine Bitters, 192
Worm Medicine for Dogs, 231

Y

Yeast—To Make, 224